THE JOY AND SORROW OF PRACTICING MEDICINE

A collection of nearly one hundred unique
interactions with the patients during fifty years
of medical practice.

by

Dr. Gholam H. Farboody

Copyright © 2018 Gholam Farboody
All rights reserved.

DEDICATION

To my late wife, Shahin, and my children,
Naseem, Nima, and Kia.

ACKNOWLEDGMENTS

I am tremendously grateful to so many people in my life, starting with my parents and my six siblings (four sisters and two brothers), all of whom supported and guided me in one way or another. I give special thanks to my sister, Akram, who was key in my receiving life-saving surgery when I was five years old. All my teachers, instructors, and mentors throughout my education from elementary school to the end of my nephrology fellowship have my greatest thanks and appreciation.

My late wife, Shahin, who unfortunately departed this world prematurely, was instrumental in my educational successes. She would stay up late at night sewing or cooking to keep *me* awake while I studied so that I'd pass the numerous exams I took during my training with distinction. These included licensure and board exams in the United States and Canada, which resulted in my being granted four different specialty board certifications in the United States and two in Canada. Like most doctor's wives, she never got a decent night's sleep as the hospital was always ringing me up, and if the hospital wasn't calling, I was at the hospital working nights. I missed special events due to my medical commitments, and I am indebted to her for the sacrifices she made on my behalf. I miss her to this day.

I am very proud of my three children, Naseem, my daughter, and Nima and Kia, my sons. They were delightful, well mannered, and obedient children and are equally delightful adults. They worked hard and tolerated my frequent absences from home due to my career. It is no surprise that not one of them became a doctor.

My coworkers and patients during different stages of my practice have been the subjects for this book and deserve my deepest gratitude.

I would like to thank Abolhassan Astaneh-Asl for his support and friendship over many decades.

My editor, Mrs. Claire M. Johnson, has been instrumental in writing this book who with her mastery of the language art she was able to convert medical terminology to laymen's terms. Her help has not been limited to the editing only, but she has been a valuable advisor to me on various aspect of publishing this book.

Finally, I would like to dedicate this book to my late wife, Shahin, and my children, Naseem, Nima, and Kia, who supported me during my long days at work and never complained.

CONTENTS

Dedication iii

Acknowledgments v

Table of Contents vii

Introduction 1

Medical School: 1963-1970 6

    Yes, It Is a Systolic Murmur 6

    Deep Sleep of An Assistant Professor 7

    Put the Pill on the Mouth of Your Uterus 8

    The Pill-in-the-Poop 9

Events During Iran Health Corp: 1970–1973 11

    Method of Self-Defense 11

    Use of Birth Control 12

    The Challenges of Vaccinating the Children of the Villagers 13

    The Story of the Corporate Office Auditor 13

    The Car Shutting Down in the Middle of a Creek 14

    Hunting with the Sergeant 15

    Celebrating Two Thousand Five Hundred Years of Civilization 15

    My First Out-of-the-Country Visit as a Doctor 16

My First Year in the United States: 1973–1974 18

    Trip to America 18

My Pediatric Rotation 22

Trying to Pick-Up Girls in Georgetown 24

Residency Training at the Cleveland Clinic: 1974–1978 25

Remain Silent If You Don't Know What to Say 25

Issues Pertaining to Security at Cleveland 26

Call Schedule for the Ohio State–Michigan Game Day 28

Winter in Cleveland 28

My Training at the University of Ottawa In Canada 1978–1982 30

Learning to Pronounce French Names 30

Diagnosing a Rare Condition 31

Meaning of Life 33

Night Call of My Neurosurgery Friend 34

A Young Lady with Very High Blood Pressure 35

Start of Private Practice as Intensivist and Nephrologist in Canada: 1982–1992 37

Older Gentleman with a Lifelong Smoking Habit 37

What About Next New Year's Eve? 38

Mr. C's Nose 39

Unexpected Diagnosis from Treatment of a Clotted Hemorrhoid 40

Events during Primary Care Practice in California: 1992–2000 43

I Want to Pee Like This 43

Authorization for Lifting Up the Testicles 44

Young Man with Pierced Genital 45

WWW. God.com 47

Returning to Home Note 48

Animal Trap 49

Genital Rash on a Woman 50

A Man with Premature Ejaculation 50

A Man with Peyronie's Disease 51

The Story of Alex 52

History of an Iranian Gentleman with a Prostate Problem with the Wife in Attendance 53

Testicular Pain Experienced by a Young Man 54

Translation Dilemma 55

Experiences During the Work as a Nephrologist: 2000–2020 57

Devil Inside the Arm 57

The Case of the Buried Penis 58

A Man with Bladder and Lung Issues 60

A Confused CNA 61

The Case of the Texas Catheter 62

How Do You Feel? 64

Pulse Oximetry 65

An Accidental Occurrence Helping to Diagnose a Condition 66

Newly Diagnosed Diabetic Man Complaining of His Diet 67

Sending Kisses while on a Breathing Machine 68

Damn Iverson 70

What Is Up? 73

Doc, Don't Bother Me, I'm Busy 74

Cheating Pacemaker 75

Doctor, Are You Married? 76

Doctor, Can You Come a Little Later? 77

Interrogation by a Woman Who Was a CIA Agent 78

The Patient I Couldn't Remember 79

The Story of My Workaholic Cardiologist Colleague 79

Kicking Marks 81

Issues of a Woman 82

The Lady with the Mysterious Touch 83

The Story of the Nurse Who Liked to Talk 83

He's the One Who Stole My Panties 84

Sign of a Stroke in a Forty-Year-Old Woman 85

My Blood Pressure Is Not the Only Thing That Goes Up ... 86

Let Me Call Doctor L. 86

Put the Mask Back On 88

The Monitor Technician Who Was Feeling Cold 88

Invention of a Homeless Man on Holding His Urine 89

Am I In the Philippines? 89

What Form of Anxiety? 90

A Language Barrier of a Foreign-Born Nurse 91

Why Wasn't It This Big When I Needed It? 93

Which Finger Is Up? 94

The Case of a Dark-Colored Worm 95

Sudden Rise of Heart Rate on the ICU Monitor 96

Number 1.5 96

Is It Raining Outside? 97

Mental Tests for Awakening a Patient from a Recent Coma ... 98

So Soft 98

Dialysis Nurse Lecturing Two Older Gay Men 99

A Lesson from My Dialysis Patient 99

Various Issues with My Marathon Running Friend 100

Additional Tales 102

Generosity of a Homeless Man 102

Prostate Check by Students in India 102
Please Stand Up When You Ask Questions 103
Dead Man Walking... 104

INTRODUCTION

My name is Dr. Gholam H. Farboody. I am a physician specializing in internal medicine and the sub-specialty of nephrology, which is kidney disease. I have been practicing medicine for nearly fifty years. During the years spent training and the many years in practice, I have come across over one hundred events that I found so interesting that I made notes of these occurrences at the time they occurred. This book is the result of my sharing of these events.

Let me first tell you about myself. I was originally born in Iran to a very lower middle-class family. I was the youngest of seven children, although several of my siblings had died at an early age for various reasons. When I was five-years old, I developed a very painful and serious medical issue. After suffering for several months with no abatement of symptoms, a surgeon agreed to operate on me even though he'd never performed this procedure on a child of my age. My family was told that I had a fifty per cent chance of dying during or shortly after surgery. Obviously, I was lucky enough to survive, but this experience affected me profoundly. During my stay in hospital, I saw the way doctors interacted with the patients and at times saved a patient's life. Even as a young child, I decided that when I grew up, I would become a doctor. At the elementary and high schools, I was always at top of my class, and when I finished high school, I took the entrance exam to only one medical school. This school was in my hometown of Tabriz as my family were unable to provide financial support for any medical schools outside Tabriz.

At that time, medical schools in Iran were accepting students from high school graduates only if they passed rigorous, extensive two-level exams. The first stage required passing the National qualifying exam for general entrance to university. In that year, only fifteen-hundred student out of over twenty-thousand participants passed the exam. I was lucky to be one of them. The second exam was administered by each school. Only those students who had passed the general exam were admitted to the second exam. Again, I was fortunate enough to pass the medical school's entrance exam as well.

Medical schools in Iran are composed of seven years of study, with the last year being an internship. Toward the end of my medical school studies, the faculty included several physicians who had trained in the United States and returned home to teach. This inspired me to seek post-doctoral training in the United States, especially in the sub-specialty of nephrology, in layman's terms "kidney disease." This decision was both professional and personal as I had experienced some issues with my kidneys.

To achieve this goal, I took a series of tests offered by the United States to Foreign Medical Graduates (called the ECFMG). The tests were intended to prove parity of medical knowledge compared with the graduates of medical schools in the United States. In addition, I had to pass an English language proficiency exam. I passed both exams, but I had to put my post-doctoral studies on hold as Iran required that I perform my mandatory military obligations before I could leave the country. In September 1970, I began my two-year stint as a doctor in the Iranian Health Corp.

By September 1972, I had completed my two years of service at the Health corps, but I had to continue working for the Health Corp and in a clinic of the Health Department because the medical training in the United States typically starts in July of every year. It wasn't until July 1973 when my internship in the United States began.

In July 1973, I arrived in the United States and started my training initially as an intern in internal medicine at Prince George's General Hospital, Cheverly, Maryland, then in pathology at Cleveland Clinic, Cleveland, Ohio, and finally I moved to Canada for additional study in internal medicine and nephrology at the University of Ottawa, Ottawa, Canada. In March of 1976, I returned to Iran to marry. We returned to the United States to complete my training.

In 1978, the Iranian Revolution and subsequent hostage crisis occurred. My visa to live in the United States during that time is known in immigration terms as a J1 visa, which was a student visa and only valid for five years. My visa was expiring. My wife was pregnant with our first child, and I did not want to return to Iran due to the instability of the country, but we couldn't stay in the United States either. I applied for additional training in Canada and was accepted. I had four more years of sub-specialty training in Canada (in internal medicine and nephrology). Upon completion of my training, I was faced with the same visa issue but this time with Canadian Government.

The Iran–Iraq war was raging at that time, and once more I was determined not to return to Iran. The only legal option I had was to work in a place in Canada where they needed a physician in my field of specialty with the stipulation that no other Canadian citizens had applied for such a position. I finally found a place in Saint John, New Brunswick. I moved my family there and started practicing in a hospital as an intensive care physician and nephrologist. Within a year, I was able to obtain permanent residency status in Canada with the assistance of the local politicians and hospital administrators. By that point, two of our three children had been born in Canada. The help and kindness of the people of Saint John was so incredible that even though I had been granted Canadian citizenship and was eligible to apply for a Green card in the United States, we decided to stay. Although we could have moved to a larger city or a university center in a more urban Canadian city, I felt obligated to remain at St. John.

Unfortunately, two years after birth of our third child, at the age of thirty-six my wife was diagnosed with stomach cancer. She underwent surgery with subsequent radiation and chemotherapy. Her diagnosis prompted me to move our family to California where my wife's brothers lived. With the help of an immigration attorney in the United States, I accepted a job offer in Los Angeles with a medical group. My wife suffered a relapse, and despite multiple attempts to treat her cancer at several well-known medical facilities, she died at age forty, only two years after moving back to the United States.

Given my desire to look after my wife prior to her death and as a single parent to my children after she died, I worked for a medical group at a nine-to-five type job so that my nights and weekends would be free for my family. Once my children were grown, I joined a group of nephrologists in Glendale, California, to practice as a kidney specialist.

What is included in this book are notes that I took of events that happened to me during my medical school years, as well as my post-doctoral training periods, and subsequent practice in Canada and California. These notes cover a period of over fifty years. Now that I have retired from practicing medicine, I believe that these events are interesting enough to be gathered in a book. All these events did occur and are mostly humorous. To protect the identity of the patients and healthcare workers mentioned in these vignettes, the names or locations of these events have been altered. I've grouped these events according to different stages of my professional life, starting with my medical school training and ending with my nephrology practice in California. I wish to mention that upon the passing of my wife, I made a conscious decision to raise my children by myself and not remarry just for the sake of having someone to look after them. I tried to make their upbringing as normal as possible by creating a fun and happy environment for them. I applied this same principle to my patients, the nursing staff, and other allied healthcare providers. Such principles meant that I experienced numerous funny events that are included herein. Not everything related is amusing, but I believe there were events that contained some valuable lessons worth reading about.

MEDICAL SCHOOL: 1963-1970

****** 1 ******

Yes, It Is a Systolic Murmur

During my fourth year of medical school, I was rotating through the internal medicine department trying to learn how to distinguish different heart sounds. A female classmate and I were in the same group listening to the heart of a patient. She believed that the patient's heart murmur was systolic, meaning that the murmur sound was happening shortly after the heart had expelled blood. Whereas I felt that the murmur was diastolic, i.e., occurring after the heart had filled with blood. (I interrupt this story to stress that the identification of the type of heart murmur is an important determinant of the location and significance of its cause).

While we argued back and forth about whether it was systolic or diastolic, our professor passed by. This man was a very well-known womanizer, and I should point out that my classmate was quite attractive. She asked this professor to listen to the patient's heart and determine who was right. The professor had his stethoscope (a tool used by doctors to listen to the heart and breath sounds) around his neck but forgot to put the earpieces on his ear. He placed the diaphragm (the other end of the stethoscope) on the patient's chest and carefully waited for a while. Then he asked my classmate what type of murmur she thought it was. She said systolic. The professor, who wouldn't have heard *any* heart sounds because he forgot to put the ear parts of the stethoscope into his ears, said: "You are right; the murmur is systolic." We both kept a straight face until he walked away, and then the two of us began laughing. Since then, anytime I've returned to Iran and visited my classmate, we laugh and joke, and still argue about what type of murmur it was.

****** 2 ******

Deep Sleep of An Assistant Professor

In the fifth year of medical school, I was rotating through Obstetrics and Gynecology. One night when I was on call, a woman in labor was admitted with a breech presentation, which normally requires Cesarean section. Neither I nor intern on call could deliver this baby. Protocol demanded that there was always an assistant professor who would sleep at the hospital and alternate the calls with two other assistant professors. The Assistant Professor who was on call that night had a reputation for being a very deep sleeper. The intern asked me to go and wake up the Assistant Professor. I knocked on the door of his room but didn't get any response. As the door was unlocked, I opened the door, entered the room, and tried to wake him up without any success. I called the intern on call, who told me that he was going to send for some help so we could wheel the Assistant Professor to the operating room, still in his bed. When the help arrived, we unlocked his bed, wheeled it into the hallway, and then into the operating room. In the operating room we parked his bed next to the bed with the woman in labor and told her that this was her surgeon. This woman, who was in severe labor pain, screamed, "Oh my God, I hope I'll survive.". Eventually we had to put a sponge soaked in cold water on his forehead to wake him up, at which point we introduced him to his patient who was lying next to him on the operating table. Fortunately, he was able to rouse himself to the point where he performed the C-section operation successfully and delivered a healthy baby.

****** 3 ******

Put the Pill on the Mouth of Your Uterus

During the OB-GYN rotation in the fifth year of medical school, students attended the clinic with a professor. One day a patient experiencing vaginal discharge was examined by the professor and found to have so-called cervicitis (infection of the cervix of the uterus). Our professor gave the woman a prescription for an antibiotic vaginal suppository containing a sulfa drug and asked her to place the suppository on the mouth of her uterus (meaning insert intravaginally and push up) twice daily. Uterus in Farsi and Arabic is called Rahem with an accent on "e". A few days later while at the same clinic, a loud knock at the door was followed by the sound of a man shouting something. Although his voice was very loud, I couldn't understand what he was saying.

The doorman came in and stated that there is a man in the outer office with swollen lips and face who was demanding to see a doctor. The professor told the doorman that this was a woman's clinic we didn't see men here. The doorman stated that the gentleman was aware of this, but the man insisted on seeing a doctor at this clinic. It was difficult to understand this man because his speech was very slurred.

My professor reluctantly agreed to let him in. As the gentleman walked in, his unusually swollen lips and face and non-comprehensible speech were obvious. After back-and-forth questioning, it became clear that this man was the husband of the lady who had been treated for a cervical infection a few days earlier. It was discovered that *his* name was Raheem, and his wife, instead of putting the vaginal suppository on the mouth of her own uterus (rahem), put the suppository on the mouth of her husband, Raheem, who was found to be allergic to sulfa drugs.

The Pill-in-the-Poop

As an intern, I treated patients at a general medicine clinic in one of the public hospitals in Tabriz. One day, one of my patients complained of having a headache for several weeks. When I tried to get his medical history, he informed me that he had visited the clinic a few weeks ago for the same problem, and I was the doctor he had seen. At that time, we did not have a good medical record-keeping capability. I did not have any record to see what medication I had prescribed to him. I asked him, "Do you know what kind of medicine I gave you?" He replied, "Not really but you gave me a pill and I took it the same day. I said, "Do you know the name of the pill that I gave you?" He said, "Well I took the pill, but the following day when I went to the bathroom to move my bowels, the pill came out with my poop. I only saw the side that was facing up, on which was printed the letters "University of Tabriz."

Apparently, the pill had not been absorbed well or the active ingredient had been absorbed but backbone material of it was so hard and non-absorbable that it had passed in his stool unaltered. As far as the name of the pill was concerned, it was on the flip side of the pill, embedded in his feces, so he was unable to determine what was the name of the pill.

EVENTS DURING IRAN HEALTH CORP: 1970–1973

****** 5a ******

Method of Self-Defense

In the first six months of our military service, all medical doctors were housed in a dormitory undergoing training similar to the training of soldiers. We received some training related to management of patients at the upcoming assignments in the villages. There were various classes offered by the army. One doctor in my group began taking karate lessons from army experts. One night at dinner, a friend of mine asked the doctor why he was taking this specific class.

He answered, "For self-defense."

My friend told him, "Listen if you want to get the best self-defense, you are better off learning how to run away fast."

I thought that was a valuable lesson.

****** 5b ******

Use of Birth Control

When I was working at the Iranian Health Corp, I had a driver, a Land Rover SUV-type car, and two assistants who were doing their two years of post-high school military service at the Health Corp. For the first six months, they were training as medical technologists, which entailed dispensing medications, giving injections, and checking vital signs. After my own six months of training, I was sent to our central station located in a small village. I was responsible for the medical care of the surrounding thirty-six villages. The care included dispensing vaccinations, family planning, and general medical care. We would visit to these villages to educate them on preventive care and family planning, in addition to providing primary care. Packed in the car we had medications for treatment as well as vaccines, birth control pills, and other medical supplies. We used to go to the capital city of the Province the first day of each month to attend seminars and replenish our supplies.

I remember a young woman who had recently gotten married but did not want to become pregnant yet. I gave her a two-month supply of birth control pill. The next month, I paid a visit to the same village and consulted with the same woman. I asked her how many pills were still left. She said she'd only used five of them and still has one full package left.

I said, "We gave the pills to you over a month ago. How come you haven't touched the second package yet?"

After a long conversation it became clear: she was using the pill only on those nights she had intercourse with her husband.

****** 5c ******

The Challenges of Vaccinating the Children of the Villagers

Our efforts at vaccinating villagers were much harder compared to handing out birth-control pills. Most of the parents tried to hide their children from us. We had to chase the kids to the top of hills, search inside the cabinets in the houses, or look inside the holes on the ground where they baked bread.

****** 5d ******

The Story of the Corporate Office Auditor

One day, an auditor from the corporate office of the Iran Health Corp visited us in our village. My assistants, who were both young men and rather mischievous, were a little afraid of the outcome of the audit. Sometimes they had dispensed medications including narcotics without documentation because we were busy at the time and then they'd forget to chart it afterward.

Our clinic was at the entrance to the village, but the village itself did not have any restaurant or grocery story. We bought our groceries from a city nearly eight miles away; we had hired a resident of the village as a cook to prepare our food.

Without telling me, my assistants added several laxatives to the auditor's food. Sometime after the meal, the auditor began to study the documentation, but he started having stomach problems and continually excused himself to go to the bathroom, as he was experiencing significant diarrhea. He excused himself and left the office shortly after the beginning of his symptoms to return to the corporate office, which was *hours* away from us by car. We didn't dare to ask him later how he made it back home; he lived in the capital city of the Province. We never found out if he suspected what happened to him when he was visiting us. We didn't ask either.

****** 5e ******

The Car Shutting Down in the Middle of a Creek

One of the villages on the periphery of our region was only accessible by a terrible road. We were responsible for visiting it once a month. At one point, the road cut across a creek bed filled shallow water. One day when we arrived at the creek, my driver did not want to cross the creek because the water was so high. But since we had already driven so far and the creek was very close to the village, I insisted on driving across. The driver eventually gave in and drove across the creek. I should have listened to him.

Unfortunately, right at the middle point of the creek bed, the car sputtered, turned off, and would not turn back on. One of my assistants eventually got out of the car and went to the village for help. Several men from the village came, got into the water, and pushed the car out of the creek. We were then able to start the car and we continued driving. I was very indebted to the villagers' assistance because I had insisted on driving across.

Interestingly, a few weeks later the sergeant who oversaw the region's security forces took me on a fishing trip. That was my first and last fishing trip I've ever been on. No fishing rod for him. He used dynamite on a pond full of fish. The sound of the blast of the dynamite paralyzed them, forcing them to come to the surface of the water. We "netted" well over one hundred fish. We took the fish to the village and divided it among the villagers, who were quite happy to have fish for dinner that night.

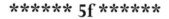

Hunting with the Sergeant

One winter day, this same sergeant invited me to go hunting for deer with him. I had never gone hunting and have not hunted since. It was a rather snowy day with patches of fog and poor visibility. After a long drive we eventually arrived at the destination, which was surrounded by mountains. First, we tried to spot deer. I saw one. He gave me his gun and I shot it. When I reached the animal to retrieve it, it wasn't a deer at all but a fox. He also was still alive. He started running, but he couldn't run fast enough. The sergeant had outfitted me with all the gear, including the glove and a heavy cover; I ran after him. When I reached him, I grabbed him from behind and held his tail, but he ran away, leaving his tail in my hand. That was the only animal we killed that day. I kept the tail for quite a while, but after remembering that injury to the fox and the numerous dead fish from the dynamite blast, I decided that neither hunting nor fishing were my cup of tea.

****** 5g ******

Celebrating Two Thousand Five Hundred Years of Civilization

My years of service at the Iranian Health Corp coincided with the celebration of two thousand five hundred years of the Persian Empire. The country celebrated for weeks. The Mayor and the governor of the region where I was stationed asked me to join them on their visit to the region and watch the celebrations with them. The region we were visiting had a large Kurdish population. Kurds have a unique style of living and dress for their holidays, which is accompanied by group dancing. At one of the events I attended, there were several couples who pulled me, the governor, and the mayor into the circle of dancers. They taught us how to dance. Well, they *tried* to teach me how to dance. I was unable to follow the dancers and disrupted their coordinated movements. It was very embarrassing!

****** 5h ******

My First Out-of-the-Country Visit as a Doctor

I was serving as a doctor in Iran Health Corp clinic in the city of Bazargan, which is on the Turkish–Iran border. One day, the Chief of the local Secret Service came to my clinic stating that I must cross the border into Turkey as the wife of one of the railroad chiefs of Turkey was sick, and they wanted an Iranian doctor to give a second opinion on the patient. This was over forty miles away.

In those days, the Secret Service of the Shah—called the "Savak"—was very powerful. You did not challenge them. I had to obey. My car, driver, two assistants, and me, along with all our medications, hit the road, accompanied by the Secret Service officer. After driving for over an hour, eventually we arrived at our destination. I attended the patient, who was the wife of the local railroad chief. I took her medical history, examined her, and ordered appropriate medications, including having my assistant inject her with antibiotics.

When we crossed the border, we found gifts with our names on them to thank us. Despite the Secret Service officer's approval, we declined the gifts, stating that our help was merely that of a friendly neighbor. This was my first time traveling outside of Iran. The second time was when I came to the United States.

MY FIRST YEAR IN THE UNITED STATES: 1973–1974

****** 6 ******

Trip to America

I had multiple problems while traveling to the United States for the first year of my internships aboard. My first few weeks of training were difficult as well. First, my visa that allowed me to live in the United States arrived six days *after* the date when I was obligated to start my training in the United States, thus, I was over a week late in arriving at my internship program. Second, the trip itself was full of mishaps. The flight that I'd booked from Tehran to the United States was held in Munich as someone was suspected of trying to smuggle drugs. We had to disembark while they searched the plane. As a result, I missed my connecting flights and was rerouted through Toronto, Canada, where I did *not* have a visa for entry. To make matters worse, while I was waiting for customs and immigration clearance from the Canadian authorities, I accidentally dropped a bottle of whiskey I had bought from a duty-free shop in Munich, creating a huge mess. I was so embarrassed.

Eventually, I was given a short-stay visa in Canada and was taken to a hotel at the airport. The following day I was picked up from my hotel and taken back to the airport and then flew to Baltimore, Maryland. In Baltimore, I called the hospital where I was supposed to train and was told to go to Washington D.C., which was closer as it was located on the border between Maryland and Washington D.C. I tried to rent a car but was told that since I did not own a credit card nor did I have a U.S. driver's license, I could not rent a car. Before I left Iran, I had purchased a light but large suitcase so I could bring all my books and belongings. As luck would have it, the handle of the luggage broke off when I attempted to bring it to the checkpoint in the Tehran Airport. In those days, suitcases did not have wheels, making it almost impossible to haul that thing around between flights. Finally, I made it to Washington D.C. and from there I hailed a taxi to take me to the hospital where I was supposed to start my internship.

The initial few weeks of the internship were even more frustrating than my flight. As I was late to start my training, the orientation week for the interns had come and gone, and I had to start working without having had any orientation. Obviously, coming from Iran, I struggled with the significantly different styles of the medical management and the language barrier. Although I had passed the English language requirement for medical school, I had great difficulty in understanding some of the accents of my patients.

It didn't stop there. I had brought some money and traveler cheques from Iran. I met another intern, who also was from Iran, and he asked me several questions about my personal and financial matters. I thought he was merely being friendly, and it was nice to talk with someone in my own language who could understand my frustrations. I told him about my money, which I had hidden inside the handle of my broken luggage as the bank refused to open an account on my name because I didn't have a social security number at that time. I was living at a hospital-owned apartment building with two other interns. Our apartment was on the ground floor of the building. As interns, we were supposed to stay at the hospital on our on-call nights.

One night this man and a visiting friend from out of state came to my apartment and had dinner with me. This night was the night before my on-call rotation was set to begin. Coincidentally, my other two roommates were on call on surgical and pediatric wards the same night while I was on-call for internal medicine. I subsequently discovered that the Iranian intern and his friend unlocked my window the night that they were my guests for dinner, entered my apartment from the window they'd unlocked, broke into my luggage, and stole all my money and traveler's checks. I later found out from his previous medical school classmates that these two had done similar burglaries back in Iran. Interestingly, they both chose psychiatry as their specialty and practiced in the United States. I started my life in the United States without a single cent. The police were unable to find any fingerprints, and I could not prove my initial suspicion.

Another embarrassing event that happened to me in the first few weeks of training was early in my training in the medical clinic and seeing patients. My first patient was a very tall African American gentleman who had a thick chart cataloguing his previous visits; I had difficulty reading the handwriting of the other doctors who had treated him. As a result, I had a hard time understanding what was wrong with him, When I asked the patient to tell me what was wrong with him but asked him to speak slowly as I wasn't a native speaker, he'd try to speak slowly for the few seconds, but then he'd begin speaking very quickly again. I could not understand him. I had to stop him and politely ask him to speak slowly, he'd repeat this cycle of speaking slowly for a few seconds, and then he'd speed up again. We did this several times. I was unable to understand what's going on with him. Attempting to summarize the patient's issue, I said, "So you have such and such problems, correct?" Suddenly he began yelling and screaming, "When did I say this?" Then door opened and several nurses rushed in to see what the problem was. I had to apologize to the gentleman and have my senior resident look after him.

On the funny side, there was an occasion where several nurses asked me where I was from and why I was late to start my internship training? I told them that I was from Iran. They asked me where was Iran located? I tried to explain that Iran was in the Middle East, and then they asked, "Do you guys have cars or only camels and donkeys." I couldn't resist. I told them that, yes, in Iran we moved around the cities by using camels and donkeys, with the camels reserved for the rich and donkeys for the poor. There was only one car in the entire country and that was owned by the Shah of Iran, but he couldn't drive his car out because when the donkeys and camels saw his car, they'd go into hysterics and utter bedlam ensured. I also told them that the reason I was late coming to the hospital was that my camel that I rode to Germany to catch my flight got pregnant in the middle of my journey, resulting in my delay on arrival to United States. They swallowed my tall tales until they checked with another Iranian resident, who told them I was pulling their legs.

****** 7 ******

My Pediatric Rotation

The first year of my internship included two months of pediatrics rotation. Several unusual things happened during this rotation.

First, there were only two interns in pediatric service when I rotated in. One week, the other intern took vacation; as a result, I had to be on call every night. In those days, there weren't any rules. Today, interns and residents are not allowed to work for more than thirty-six hours straight. I had to cover pediatrics regardless of the call I took at night. I was supposed to be on call every day and night for a week. On the third night, where I hadn't slept for two days, a child was brought in, feverish and sleepy, with a stiff neck. I suspected meningitis. To confirm my diagnosis demanded that I perform a lumbar puncture to obtain spinal fluid. You insert a needle in the spinal canal to analyze the fluid. When I tried to start the procedure, I found I couldn't hold the syringe steady enough to numb the skin of the child. I had to call my staff man to ask him to do the procedure for me. My hands were shaking from exhaustion.

Another interesting case that occurred during my pediatric rotation had to do with a child of about seven years old whom I admitted to the hospital for presenting bloody stools. Following admission, he stayed in hospital for a couple of days, during which time I had several pleasant interactions with him and his parents. He wouldn't allow anyone to perform blood-draws or let them X-ray him unless I was present, or he'd been told that I had ordered the test. We had to do a barium enema X-ray on him as those days we did not have capability of doing colonoscopy on children. I remember I had to go with him to the radiology department for the test. He was subsequently discharged. A few weeks later he was seen as an outpatient by my staff man in his office. I had a call from my staff man asking me if I were available at some point to hold the hand of the child at the X-ray department as he needed a second barium enema for comparison with the first one. He was Chief of Pediatrics in the hospital. He asked me to apply for pediatric residency at a famous university-affiliated hospital where he also had working privileges. I told him I was honored, but that I found it difficult treating sick children.

I had a somewhat similar situation with a hospital administration secretary whose husband was an active U.S. Army veteran and was on duty out of the country. The secretory was pregnant, and the husband was not available at the time of labor and delivery. She had asked the obstetrician to call me to see if I could be present in the labor and delivery room when she went into labor, even though at the time I was still working in pediatrics. I obliged.

I was unmarried throughout my internship but was dating a nurse who worked in the internal medicine unit. One day I was presenting a case to a GI doc. He said to me that he understood I was dating this young woman. I replied, "Yes I am." This was in the middle of my internship, and I had begun searching for a residency program for the following year. He asked me if I'd ask my girlfriend to attend a party on his private yacht by herself (without me), then he would find a residency program for me at a nearby prestigious hospital for the following year. I politely declined his request. A few months later, the same girlfriend accompanied another staff man on a vacation in Florida. She brought back lots of gifts for me, which I refused.

Obviously, our relationship ended right there and then. I'm still upset with myself that I declined the GI man's request. If she had gone to his party, I might have had a very different future and a choice of training programs. What a fool I was.

****** 8 ******

Trying to Pick-Up Girls in Georgetown

A few months after I had started my internship, three of my Iranian colleagues, who also were interns or residents, suggested we go for a night out to Georgetown, which is downtown of Washington, D.C. and only six miles away from our hospital. One of my friends, who had been in the area for the previous two years and was familiar with the region, stated that he wanted to try to look for some girls to go barhopping with. Interestingly, four women happened to be standing on the corner of the intersection where we were standing. With bravado, my friend said that he had this covered. He went over to speak to them, returning after a few minutes. The women said to go to this bar within the walking distance from where we were standing, and they would join us there. Naturally, we were quite excited and made a beeline for the bar. When we arrived, to our surprise there weren't any women in the bar. After a little while we realized that the ladies had tricked us, and this was a gay bar. We went back to the intersection to confront them, but they'd disappeared.

RESIDENCY TRAINING AT THE CLEVELAND CLINIC: 1974–1978

****** 9 ******

Remain Silent If You Don't Know What to Say

While training in pathology one day, I was responsible for the so-called frozen section desk at the operating room. The pathologist in the frozen section receives a tissue sample from the operating room when the surgeon needs an immediate answer about the tissue to determine whether it is cancerous or not.

In this case, a tissue sample was brought in by a surgeon. I immediately processed the tissue and took it to my staff man, who was a very wise and soft-spoken gentleman. I put the slide on the double-headed microscope. The staff man moved the slide, scrutinizing it while I was watching the slide with him. The surgeon stood next to us waiting for us to determine whether the tissue was cancerous or not. If it were cancerous, then he had to return to the operating room and make a further excision of the area to make sure that no cancerous tissue was left behind. If the tissue was not cancerous, then he could return to the surgical theater and close-up incision site.

Nearly two minutes of silence passed while my professor scanned the tissue. I was studying the slide with him; both the surgeon and me were impatient for an answer. I felt I had to speak. "Well, what is it? What is it?" He did not reply. Another minute or two passed in silence. Again, I jumped in saying, "Well, what do you think what it is?". My staff man was still screening the slide. Finally, he spoke. Before giving his diagnosis, he said to me. "What I'm saying now may have a major impact on your life in the future. When you are not sure what you are seeing or what to say, you are better off to stay silent because if you say something wrong or inappropriate, you will have to take it back later. It is far better to say nothing and remain noncommittal than retracting your statements later. Try to analyze what you have to say or do before you act."

I have kept my wise professor's advice in mind since then and usually try to follow it.

****** 10 ******

Issues Pertaining to Security at Cleveland

An infectious disease staff man used to make early morning rounds, usually at five to six am, and then would leave the hospital late in the evening. The residents who were rotating through his service would often stay in the hospital every night, regardless of whether they were going to be on call that night or not. They had to see the patients before the staff man started making rounds, which would be something like four am. Although the hospital had 24-7 security with a mobile patrol that policed the hospital's parking lots, during the four years I was at the clinic, this particular staff man had been mugged three times. He always carried a $50 bill in his wallet, and whenever he was held either at gun point or with another type of weapon, he'd hand over his $50 bill and was let go.

Another event I remember involves a colleague training with me. As he was getting married, we had arranged to throw him a bachelor party at a strip club. When it came time to leave the bar, we decided to walk out together as a group. Our groom friend told us that he'd decided to stay for a bit. He was from the area and was sure he'd be safe. We all left, leaving the man of honor at the bar. The following day when we got to the hospital, we found out that our soon-to-be married friend had been admitted to the hospital. He was in the intensive care unit and on a ventilator. After leaving the bar, he'd been beaten up. He recovered quickly with no residual injuries and was married on schedule.

We residents had been told by the hospital administration that if we were at home and called into the clinic late at night, we should drive through the intersection of Euclid Avenue and East 105th without stopping, even if the light was red. I should point out that at that time, the East 105th and Euclid intersection was in an extremely high crime area to the point that even the police often avoided it. The hospital had told us that if we received a traffic ticket, they would pay for it. In those days, there was no reporting of such violations to the DMV or such violations having any adverse effect on the car insurance premiums or one's driving record.

****** 11 ******

Call Schedule for the Ohio State–Michigan Game Day

Ohio State University and University of Michigan have long-standing history of rivalry and camaraderie. There was always an issue about who was going to work on game day; nobody volunteered. The solution that the clinic came up with to solve this problem was to install the largest screen TV available in those days. From then on, there was a fight over who volunteered to be on-call on game day because everybody wanted to work. The hospital placed the TV screen in a high-capacity room and provided snacks and drinks on the game day so everyone could attend. It was frequently jammed with the people.

****** 12 ******

Winter in Cleveland

Toward the end of my training in Cleveland, there was an unusually harsh winter with a so much snow that the city ran out of the money for plowing the snow and spraying the salt on the roads. On a day when the weather forecast called for blizzard conditions with the snow beginning in the morning, I eventually arrived at the hospital for work. Based on worsening weather and considering the weather forecast for rest of the day, the clinic offered the medical staff and residents the option of either staying overnight at a nearby hotel where the cost would be absorbed by the clinic or leaving the hospital early before the roads became impassable. I left the hospital at about 1 p.m. In those days I lived in the city of Euclid, which was located on the shores of Lake Erie. On a normal day, it would take about twenty minutes to get to the clinic. On that day, it took me six hours to get home. Cars were lined up one after another on the freeway on ramps. Drivers were out of their cars and, in a group, pushing forward the car in the front of the line forward so it could get on the freeway, thus opening up the road for the car behind it to enter the freeway next. I stayed home the following day as I was unable to drive to the hospital.

MY TRAINING AT THE UNIVERSITY OF OTTAWA IN CANADA 1978–1982

****** 13 ******

Learning to Pronounce French Names

When I started my internal medicine residency training in Canada, my first rotation was in the field of endocrinology. My first assignment in endocrinology was attending in the thyroid clinic. The exam protocol for residents had us enter the waiting room, call out the patient's name, take them to the examining room, take their medical history, and then perform a physical exam. Once the exam was finished, we conferred with the staff man to report the findings, discuss the patient's problem, and come up with a plan to manage their treatment.

The chart of my first patient was handed to me by the nursing staff. I was told to go to the waiting room and call the patient. I took the chart and went to the waiting room and called out the patient's name: "Mrs. "LEEBLANK." Nobody answered. "Mrs. Leeblank," I said, but louder, and still there was no response. I returned to the nursing station and told the nurse the patient wasn't in the waiting room. She looked at me and looked at the waiting room from a distance, and said, "She's there. How did you say her name?" I said, "Miss Leeblank" She laughed and said, "Go back and say Miss. Loblan." In French, this is written as Leblanc. I returned to the waiting room and as soon as I said, "Miss Loblan," one lady stood up and said," Oui," which means "yes" in French. That was my first introduction to French pronunciations.

****** 14 ******

Diagnosing a Rare Condition

By the time I left Cleveland, I had completed the full pathology training course and had obtained American board certification in pathology. For a variety of reasons, including the ongoing problem with my visa in the U.S., I decided to change my specialty. I enjoyed interacting with live patients as opposed to microscopes. I always had an interest in becoming a kidney specialist. Once in Canada, I opted to change my specialty and take more training in internal medicine and then nephrology (the field of kidney function).

When I was rotating through hematology/oncology a young man with lymph-node enlargement and abnormal blood-test results was referred to our service at the hospital. I had done a few bone marrow aspiration and biopsies during my training in pathology. With the signed consent of the patient, I obtained samples from the bone marrow in the form of aspiration of the content of the bone marrow, as well as a core of the bone tissue for further analysis. The following day, I accompanied other residents to the Pathology Department to look at the bone marrow aspiration. The pathologist, who had a double-headed microscope, placed us on one side and himself on the other side, began scanning the slide. After several minutes, he stated that he was unable to determine the exact cause of the abnormality of the bone marrow, and we would have to wait for bone marrow biopsy results, which would take a few days.

However, since I hadn't had a chance to look at the slide with the pathologist, I asked him if he could look at the slide with me as well; he agreed. While he was scanning the slide, I noticed that there is one white blood cell that seemed to have a red blood cell in it. There was a new disease entity that had been identified just a few months earlier toward the end of my training at the Cleveland Clinic, the hallmark of which was the presence of red blood cells within the macrophage—a kind of white blood cell.

I asked the pathologist to scan the slide further to see if more similar cells could be found. There were similar cells present. I said to the pathologist, "I now know what the diagnosis is." He looked at me in surprise and said, "What is it?" I told them that the patient was suffering from HMR, which stands for Histiocytic Medullary Reticulosis. He said he never heard of it, and the other residents agreed with him. So did the staff man, who stated that there was no such thing. I had not told anyone that I was a certified pathologist.

In those days, we did not have Google. The following day I went to the hospital's library to search for references to support my diagnosis. It became clear that this is a form of lymphoma. Since then, the disease has been renamed and has broadened its category to include many other conditions. The new name is: HLH (Hemophagocytic LymphoHistiocytosis), clearly a mouthful. This became a case for presentation at what used to be called the Grand Round. This was one of the few occasions where I was able to use my pathology background to make a diagnosis that stumped everyone else. Since then, I have used my pathology background to make diagnoses on biopsies of the kidney, as well as hematology/oncology problems that I have faced. In the long run, it was worth going through that additional training. It gave me a depth of medical knowledge that has proved to be invaluable.

****** 15 ******

Meaning of Life

As the senior resident in internal medicine, the emergency room referred a patient to me who appeared to have suffered a heart attack. He was a 48-year-old male who was admitted with severe chest pain. The patient was transferred to the ICU, and while in the ICU, he developed severe arrhythmia of the heart, accompanied by a complete heart block along with a drop in blood pressure. Restoring the rhythm of his heart required installing a temporary pacemaker, which I did. Unfortunately, even with the pacemaker he went into ventricular fibrillation—a too rapid heart rate and we had to defibrillate the patient. We were successful in bringing him back to life, but overnight despite giving various kinds of medications to the patient to prevent recurrence of ventricular fibrillation, he continued having recurrent episodes and eventually after several resuscitative efforts, he did not respond to the last go around and died.

In the morning on the ward round, my professor asked me to report the events of the previous night, and it was obvious that I was upset. The professor asked me if I could show him all the electrocardiograms and subsequent tracing of the heart while the patient was in the ICU. He reviewed all the tracing and medications that I had given, as well as the pacemaker-related tracing of the heart rhythm showing the proper function of the pacemaker. Finally, he turned to me and said, "I know you are upset, but you have to know that you did your best, and I don't see any problem with your management." He then proceeded to quote a philosopher—I don't know his name—who said, "Life is a lethal disease sexually transmitted."

****** 16 ******

Night Call of My Neurosurgery Friend

During my residency, I lived in an apartment building next to the hospital. There was an underground connection between the hospital and the apartment building. The apartment building had an outside staircase as an escape route in event of fire. One night, an emergency neurosurgery case came to the hospital, and my friend, who was a neurosurgery senior resident, was sleeping at home when he was called by the emergency room to attend to a patient immediately. My friend who had answered the phone seemed to have fallen back asleep while talking on the phone. The ER doctor kept trying to talk to my friend but got no answer. The ER doctor figured out that my friend had fallen back to sleep while holding the handset of the phone. Further paging was unsuccessful, and the phone call did not go through as my friend had not yet hung up the phone. The ER doctor had no option but to ask security to go to his apartment and wake him up. They tried to get into the building from inside and knocked vigorously on the door but were unable to awaken my friend. So, they went from outside through the outside stairs to this resident's apartment. To their surprise, the window was open, they entered the apartment from the window and then went to my friend's bedroom, who was still sleeping. They began shaking him to wake him up. Suddenly he woke up and was naturally surprised to see the security guard in the room. The resident still had the telephone set in his hand. Now fully awake, he accompanied the security guard to the emergency room, where they had to perform emergency surgery on the patient to drain the blood from his head. The surgery was successful.

****** 17 ******

A Young Lady with Very High Blood Pressure

A very attractive twenty-one-year-old female was referred to our service at nephrology for having intractable high blood pressure and abnormal urine tests. Further work up revealed that she had lupus erythematosus, which is a serious systemic disease affecting multiple organs, including the kidneys. Her blood pressure required multiple medications to keep it under control. In those days we used to prescribe a medication called Minoxidil to patients with intractable high-blood pressure. This medicine is still in use and is marketed in liquid form under the name of Rogaine, which is for hair growth for men. When this medicine is given by mouth, it is a very effective. Unfortunately, it also causes excessive hair growth in undesirable locations. After a few weeks of use, this patient the young lady began to grow hair on her face to the point that she had to schedule frequent trips to beauticians for electrolysis. Her hair growth became so excessive, we couldn't see inside her ear canals because of excessive hair growth inside her ears. We stopped the Minoxidil, but as soon as we did, her blood pressure shot up, and her kidney function worsened; we had to restart her on Minoxidil. At the time that I left the service, she was alive but suffered kidney problems and was having electrolysis twice a week for hair removal. She agreed to keep on taking Minoxidil because of her extremely high blood pressure, which could not be controlled by any other medication combinations at that time.

START OF PRIVATE PRACTICE AS INTENSIVIST AND NEPHROLOGIST IN CANADA: 1982–1992

****** 18 ******

Older Gentleman with a Lifelong Smoking Habit

One of my early patients in Canada when I first started practicing was an 80-year-old man who was admitted to the hospital with a heart attack. Per protocol, I asked him for his history and whether he smoked or had smoked at any point in his life. He said yes, he did. He'd been a smoker for seventy-five years. I said, "Wait a minute. For how many years?" He replied, "Seventy-five." I said, "You're eighty years old. How can you have a seventy-five-year history of smoking?" He said, "When I was in the first grade of elementary school, the teacher kicked me out of class because he caught me smoking and called my parents both of whom were also smokers, and their cigarettes were my source of supply.

****** 19 ******

What About Next New Year's Eve?

One day, a forty-four-year-old man was brought in by ambulance with cardiac arrest. His wife was a nurse and had initiated basic cardiopulmonary resuscitation as soon as the patient had lost consciousness following a complaint of severe chest pain. The paramedics were called, and they continued CPR until the ambulance arrived at the emergency room. The emergency room doctors discovered he'd gone into ventricular fibrillation. They defibrillated him with electric shock, which resumed his heart rhythm, and he regained consciousness. He began to talk and was coherent. He had several other heart rhythm issues that night. I put a temporary pacemaker on him at the stroke of midnight on New Year's Eve. He asked me, "Hey doc, what do you think we will be doing and where we will be next New Year's Eve?" He recovered and was discharged.

I remember he gave me a nice leather folder on the day of his discharge, which I have kept and still use frequently. Unfortunately, he had another cardiac arrest at home six months after his discharge and died. After his death, his wife wrote me a letter, thanking me for giving her six more months of life with her husband. I still remember his face whenever I use his folder. Unfortunately, he was not able to celebrate the following year's New Year's Eve.

****** 20 ******

Mr. C's Nose

A seventy-three-year-old Jewish man was brought in by paramedics with a heart attack; his wife accompanied him. I attended him shortly after his arrival and spent all night trying to stabilize him; he was experiencing a variety of heart rhythm issues. Around five in the morning, I felt that his condition has stabilized enough that I could return home to take a shower and be ready to take my children to school. I went home, made coffee, drank two cups of it, took a shower, and then dropped my children off at school.

When I returned to the hospital to make my rounds, I started with the coronary care unit. I arrived at Mister C's bed and asked him how he was doing. Suddenly his wife, who was at his bedside, said, "What are we going to do with his nose?" I looked at Mr. C.'s nose; it was rather big, I must admit. I said to his wife, "Mrs. C, you were here all night. You know what we went through and how much of a problem we had. This is not the time to talk about his nose. Granted, he could benefit from a nose job, but this is something that can be done sometime in the future." The wife started laughing loudly and then said, "What do you mean, Doctor? I'm not talking about plastic surgery." I asked, "Then what are you talking about?". She replied, "The oxygen tube that was placed in his nose is causing his nose it to bleed. That's what I meant." We all had a good laugh.

****** 21 ******

Unexpected Diagnosis from Treatment of a Clotted Hemorrhoid

A thirty-eight-year-old overweight female teacher came into the emergency room complaining of severe rectal pain from a hemorrhoid. The ER doctor examined her and determined that the blood inside her hemorrhoids appeared to have become clotted, which was causing her pain. Essentially, a hemorrhoid is a dilated vein in the rectal area and sometimes the blood inside the hemorrhoid clots and causes pain. The standard treatment for that would be incision of the vein to squeeze out the clot, which provides prompt relief.

Following administration of topical anesthesia, the ER doctor made the incision and began to expel the clotted blood. In doing so, he did a rectal exam, trying to squeeze out the remainder of the clot. While performing this procedure, he noticed that she has something very hard behind the front wall of rectum, between the rectum and the abdomen. He asked the patient about whether she has had any issues with her menstruation. She replied that she hadn't menstruated in several months, but that was normal for her. He ordered an ultrasound of her abdomen and pelvis. To his surprise, the patient was pregnant, and the hard object he was feeling was the head of the fetus. The patient was referred to the OB physician and soon after that, she gave birth to a baby. It became a joking and a teasing point for us that any woman who wants to be pregnant should have a rectal exam by Dr M. (the emergency room doctor), and those who don't want to be pregnant, should not allow Dr M to do a rectal exam on them!

****** 22 ******

Healing Hands

After ten years of practicing medicine at St John New Brunswick, we decided to move to California because of multiple factors, but the key issue was my wife's health issues. At the goodbye party given by the hospital and colleagues, a physician partner of mine, who shared the care for ICU and CCU patients with me, gave a speech. He claimed that I have healing hands, and that they were going to miss my healing hands. He then proceeded to mention an event that had happened a few months earlier. One day, I had a patient in the coronary care unit, who was what we called a DNR, meaning do not resuscitate. Although very alert and coherent, she was about eighty years old and had severe heart failure. She had provided us with a legally executed will that she did not want to be resuscitated or placed on any artificial life support if her heart stopped.

One morning I was on my way to the hospital when I got a page to call the coronary care unit immediately. In those days we did not have cell phones. I got off the freeway, even though I was very close to the hospital, and found a payphone to call the coronary care unit. They told me that this patient had just developed a very slow heart rate on the monitor and had stopped breathing. I told them that I was very close to the hospital, and I'd be there in a few minutes. They told me that my partner (the speaker at the party) was there and was willing to pronounce her dead. I said that's okay then, went back to my car, drove to the hospital, and parked. I went up to the coronary care unit.

When I entered the unit, I saw my partner along with the nurses standing around the patient's bed; they had turned off her cardiac monitor. I asked what had happened. They told me that she had been alert, awake, and had been receiving oxygen. Suddenly her heart rate slowed down on the monitor, and then she stopped breathing and became unresponsive. Dr R. assessed the patient, noticing that she had no spontaneous breathing or palpable pulse, and placed a note on the chart pronouncing her dead. While I was listening to them, I accidentally put my hand over the patient's foot. Suddenly a loud noise came from the patient, and she started breathing. We turned on the cardiac monitor noticing that her heart rhythm had returned. She then woke up and had a large meal for lunch that day. Unfortunately, the following day she died. My partner, who'd put the note on the chart stating that the patient had died, immediately grabbed the chart of the patient and crossed out his note, stating that it was an error. I assumed that my walk prior to standing next to the patient's bedside had generated some electricity on my body, which was discharged on the patient when I touched her foot, acting like an electric shock. My answer to my friend's comment about my healing hand was that my hand was good only for twenty-four hours.

EVENTS DURING PRIMARY CARE PRACTICE IN CALIFORNIA: 1992–2000

****** 23 ******

I Want to Pee Like This

While acting as a primary care provider, my colleague, who was also a primary care provider but female, referred to me this Asian man who was reluctant to have a female doctor examining him and discussing his issues with him. The patient was in his early fifties but whose English was limited. He was accompanied by his wife, who was quite fluent in English. After the interview—where his wife was quite helpful— I discovered that he might have an enlarged prostate. I asked the wife to step out of the exam room, and I did a rectal exam. He did, indeed, have an enlarged prostate. I gave him some samples of a medication that is a standard blood-pressure medication (in the class of what are known as alpha blockers), but they also help the urine flow of the patients with enlarged prostates. I ordered some blood tests and gave a package of the medication to the patient, explained how to take the medication (using his wife to translate), and asked him to come back in one month to tell me if the medication was helpful or not.

One month later the patient showed up but this time unaccompanied by his wife. I asked him how he was doing? He said, "Good and bad." I asked, "What do you mean?" He said, "When I came to you, I peed like this." He went to the faucet in the exam room and opened it slightly to the point of dripping. "You gave me medicine. I took medicine. I now pee," he opened the faucet a little more, "Like that." I said, "That's good!" He said, "No, no. I want to pee-pee like this," and he opened the faucet so that the water was at full strength, gushing out of the spigot. I laughed a lot and asked for a urology referral.

****** 24 ******

Authorization for Lifting Up the Testicles

During the first ten years of my practice in the United States, I worked for an HMO organization where we had to request authorization for specialty referrals. A couple in their seventies came to me one day asking me to place an authorization for surgical lifting of the husband's testicles. I asked them what was the problem? The wife said that the husband's testicles were hanging down so low that it was causing serious hygienic problems. When I asked what you mean? She stated that whenever her husband went to have a bowel movement, he had to lift up his testicles because they were hanging so low that they reached the water in the toilet. They had lowered the water in their toilet water, but his testicles still touched the water. They wanted to have a procedure done to life up his testicles, so they were closer to his penis. In an attempt to obtain authorization for this surgery, I had to have a photograph of the patient taken in a position to show his knees in the front, with the hanging scrotum in between, and then submit this photograph to the authorization committee for surgical referral. Sadly, even though authorization for the procedure was granted, but the gentleman had a stroke before we could do the surgery.

****** 25 ******

Young Man with Pierced Genital

When I looked at the office schedule for the next patient that I was supposed to see, I noticed that the patient had stated that he has a personal problem and had refused to mention his problem to the front office and nurse when he checked in. When I went in to see the patient and asked him what the matter was, he stated that he had a problem with his genitals. I asked him what kind of problem? Looking both depressed and ashamed, he admitted that he had pierced his penis last week, and now the tip of his penis was painful and swollen. The patient was in his early thirties, and the executive officer of a major company in our neighborhood.

I asked him pull down his pants and underwear, which revealed that his penis was the size of a small baseball bat. When I tried to squeeze the tip of the penis where a ring was hanging, a significant amount of pus extruded from the site. It was obvious that this exam was causing him a lot of pain. He then asked me, "Hey doc what's going to happen'?' I jokingly said to him, "Before I answer your question, please tell me, were you able to make a home run with this bat? Have you lost your mind, man? What is this? It looks like a baseball bat." He started to cry. He asked, "Is it going to fall off?" I told him no, that we're going to get a culture of the discharged material and give him an empiric antibiotic to start immediately, subject to a possible change of antibiotic when culture results became available. I assured him that the antibiotics would likely bring down the swelling and infection, but it would be a good idea to have the ring removed ASAP to facilitate healing. He dried his tears and attempted to give me a hug. When I said no keep the hug until next week for the recipient of the hopefully healed bat. He smiled and shook my hand and left.

****** 26 ******

Young Swiss Girl with Gastroenteritis

A young lady from Switzerland was brought into my office by her American boyfriend. While visiting him, she had experienced severe vomiting and diarrhea for the preceding three days. She was extremely weak and dehydrated. Her boyfriend stated that he kept telling her to drink water, but she refused, stating that she has never had a glass of water in her life. I clearly was surprised by this response and asked her since she didn't drink water, what *did* she drink? She stated that water had no taste, and she preferred drinking something which did have taste. I started her on an intravenous drip containing sugar and salt (which is called dextrose and normal saline). I jokingly told her that I was sorry that I could not add sparkling water to her IV fluid but that she was receiving tasty sweet and salty fluid through her veins. She laughed.

****** 27 ******

WWW. God.com

Muhammad was a Muslim Arab–American in his fifties who was my patient for few years. He was married to a very pleasant Caucasian American woman, and they had a daughter in her late teen years. They often visited me together. One day they came into my office, with Muhammad vomiting and in agony from severe back pain. On the day when he visited me, it was during Ramadan, which also coincided with the Christmas season. I suspected that he had a kidney stone. At that clinic we had an X-ray facility and a small laboratory. I ordered a urine test and a plain X-ray of the abdomen. His urine test showed that he had blood in his urine, and the X-ray showed a small shadow, which is an indication of a kidney stone. I told him and his family that this shadow was most likely a kidney stone. His wife mentioned that Muhammad was fasting for Ramadan. Given his present condition, should he continue with his fasting or not? I replied, "He should not be fasting at all." Muhammad jumped in and said, "Says who?" I replied, "Says me." "Who are you?" he replied. I said, "I'm your doctor." He said, "Do you know what kind of requirement you need to have in order to avoid fasting in Ramadan?" I said, "Yes. He then said, "What?" I said, "The order of your doctor." He sneered at me and said, "Oh, yes, and what do you know about Ramadan?" I said, "I happened to be born to Muslim parents. I am technically a Muslim." He said, "Yes, but you are chewing gum." In Ramadan, Muslims are not supposed to drink, eat, or chew gum during daylight. As I was caught red handed, I said, "But I am a religious person who believes in God, and I believe that there is only one god to whom all religions pray to. I do that by going to the www.God.com website every night." He and his family laughed. Next, I proceeded to tell them why he should avoid fasting in his case: because of the kidney stone, he needed to drink a lot of fluid so he could flush his kidneys and hopefully push out the kidney stone.

At this point, someone knocked on the door of the examination room. It was my nurse telling me that one of my patients, who did not have any appointment and was not sick, had brought me a gift for Christmas along with a card. I hold her to leave the gift on my desk and asked her to wait until I read the card. I opened the card to see who the card was from? When I read the note, I showed the card to Muhammad's wife and asked her to read it out loud. "Merry Christmas, Doctor. I just want to thank you for taking great care of me and giving my life back to me. I hope you will have a happy New Year, signed Jesus." I said to them, "See, even Jesus is thanking me." They all laughed. I proceeded to put Muhammad on an IV drip and administered some pain medicine. Once the IV was finished, he could go home with the instructions to drink lots of fluid and NO fasting until stones had passed. He agreed. I referred him to a Urologist for follow up.

****** 28 ******

Returning to Home Note

One day I saw a forty-year-old lady, who had a runny nose and a sore throat. She stated that her husband had sent her to see her doctor and had threatened her that if she didn't see a doctor, he would not let her back into the house. She wanted some proof of the doctor's office visit. After I examined her, it became clear that she was suffering from nothing more than a common cold. So, I wrote a note on the office letterhead addressed to her husband. The note went like this: Dear Honorable Sir: Your wife, Mrs. RD, was seen today at this clinic. She is suffering from a common cold for which no prescription antibiotic is required. She however can be contagious. Please allow her back to the house. It is advisable to have a night or two sleeping separately as she is sick. She is probably better off staying in the master bedroom while you sleep downstairs on the couch. A few days later, I got a card from the husband thanking me that said: "I followed the Doctor's advice. Permission granted !!!"

****** 29 ******

Animal Trap

A gentleman in his late sixties came to the clinic stating that he'd injured himself at his farm. Upon questioning, it became clear that he had accidentally stepped on an animal trap that he'd set up sometime earlier. Although I am not sure how the trap functioned, clearly something went through his pants between his thighs, injuring his scrotum. When I asked him to drop his pants so I could discern at what kind of injury he had sustained, it became clear that he had a wide-open cut on his scrotum where his testicles were hanging out, and not covered by any skin. He did not complain about having significant pain, and there was no bleeding on the site either. I sent him back to the emergency room to have the cut surface lavaged with the sterile fluid, and the scrotum openings sutured closed.

****** 30 ******

Genital Rash on a Woman

A lady in her forties came into the office complaining of having a rash on her private area. Upon examination, it became clear that the rash was so-called a vesicular (blister kind) rash suspicious for herpes. Upon further questioning, it became clear that she was having an extra-marital affair. Her partner had performed oral sex on her, resulting in the development of the rash. She asked me what she story could tell her husband that did not reveal her extra-marital affair. I did not have any honest answer other than what I told her: the rash was herpes and most likely related to oral herpes caused by transmission from the mouth of the partner. Antiviral medications for topical as well as systemic use were prescribed, and she was advised to avoid further contact with the same partner.

****** 31 ******

A Man with Premature Ejaculation

I saw in my office a man in his forties who was complaining of premature ejaculation. At that time, one of the medications used for such patients were drugs under the category of anti-depressant class of medications called SSRIs. A prescription for Zoloft was provided and advice was given. Few weeks later the patient came back stating that the medication did not help. I asked him if he had been taking the medication every day? He stated that he only was taking it on the days that he was having intercourse. I asked him how long before intercourse did he take the Zoloft? He said right at the time of intercourse. I said, "That's the reason it hasn't worked. You need to take it at the same time every day so that the drug can be absorbed into your system. The level of the drug in your body needs to remain steady to be effective in alleviating your premature ejaculation." He then said, "Doc, you mean I have to take it by mouth and take it daily?" I said yes. He then smiled and said that he had been putting the pill on the tip of his penis upon the penetration during the sex. Obviously, this was the source of his problem. This demonstrates how a short period of interaction with the patient created by the requirement of seeing a certain number of patients per day can cause inadequate communication with the patients.

A Man with Peyronie's Disease

I referred a gentleman in his thirties with Peyronie's disease to a urologist. This condition is characterized by curvature of the erected penis. A few weeks after this referral, the patient came back for a follow-up. Upon questioning, he stated that when he saw the urologist, the urologist asked him to take a picture of his penis when erect and give it to him so he could submit the photography to the HMO for authorization for surgery. The patient claimed that he had to purchase a polaroid camera for this purpose, took a picture of his erect penis, and submitted that to the urologist's office. Based on the photograph, the authorization was granted by the utilization committee of the HMO. He did not come back for follow-up with me after the surgery to see how the surgery went, so I do not know if the surgery was successful or not.

****** 33 ******

The Story of Alex

Alex was an eighty-four-year-old Latino widower who lived in an assisted living facility. One day he came to my office complaining that he was lonely and depressed. Alex was hard of hearing, and I had to talk very loudly to he could hear me. His medical issues were limited to arthritis and high blood pressure. When I asked him why he was lonely given he lived in a facility with a lot of residents? He stated that, "Yes he had been approached by a lot of ladies at the assisted living place." I asked him if he wasn't interested in women. He said he had a lot of interest in women, but the women in the assisted living facility were old. I asked him if there were any women in their sixties. He said yes, but they were too old. Then I asked him what did he want? He said, "I am looking for a woman in her forties." I said, "Alex, you are eighty-four-years-old and you're looking for a lady in her forties?" He said yes. Then I said, "I'm sorry. You must look for it yourself. I cannot help you in this regard."

He always had refused to wear a hearing aid. After discussing his blood pressure and hearing problems, I prescribed him some antidepressant and renewed his arthritis medications. All conversations between the two of us consisted of me shouting at him so he could hear me. After giving instructions regarding his medications, I said goodbye to him and asked him to make a follow up appointment. I left the room and picked up the chart for the next patient, who was waiting for me in an exam room right next to the room where I'd treated Alex. She was a harpist in her forties. As soon as I entered the room, she raised a pointed finger at me and said, "Don't you dare to talk to me about Alex." She had already heard every word I'd said to Alex. I smiled and assured her that I wasn't going to talk to her about him.

****** 34 ******

History of an Iranian Gentleman with a Prostate Problem with the Wife in Attendance

My colleague who used to work in the same office as I referred a gentleman of Iranian descent who was ashamed to be examined by a female doctor for his urinary problem. I agreed to see the patient, who came to the office with his wife. The time of the visit also coincided with the Iranian New Year. The gentleman who was in his early seventies was a very pleasant soft-spoken man. I started asking questions about the pattern of voiding that he had been having. I asked him how many times a night did he wake up to go to the bathroom to urinate? Before he opened his mouth to answer, his wife said three times. Then I asked him if when he went to the bathroom to urinate, did the urine come out right away or did he have to wait a while before it started to flow? His wife responded that it came right away. Then I asked if the urine flow was steady or a dribble? She said it was steady. Finally, I asked if the urine stream was quite narrow or normal, and again the wife jumped in and said it was a normal stream.

I then looked at the wife and asked her if she accompanied the husband every time he went to the bathroom to urinate and she replied no. Then I asked, "How do you know how he urinates then?" They both laughed and the husband, who'd been mostly quiet up until then, said that she had been a spokesperson for both of them throughout their marriage. I asked how long had they been married? She said forty-two years. I then turned to the man and told him that I don't believe the answers that your wife gave me. "I think you might have problems with your prostate; however, I will ask your wife to step out so I can check your prostate. Before I do so, I want to wish you a happy Iranian New Year. I also want to let you know that I will send you a greeting card for New Year and will likely mention to you that I may nominate you to the Persian equivalent of Time Magazine Man of the Year for tolerating such a woman for forty-two years." They both laughed.

My examination of his prostate revealed that he had significant enlargement of the prostate. I gave him a one-month supply of medication, which is a blood-pressure medicine but improves urination flow on men as well (in the alpha blocker category of blood-pressure medications) and asked him to come back in a month to tell me if it worked. I also ordered some related screening lab tests. The following month they came back for a follow-up appointment. However, the wife, still their spokesperson, complained that the husband had told the family what I told them on the previous visit, and now she couldn't speak any more at home as anytime she opens her mouth to talk, all of their family members began laughing.

****** 35 ******

Testicular Pain Experienced by a Young Man

I saw at the clinic a young Latino man who was complaining of pain in his testicles. He also was experiencing shortness of breath. While he was sitting on the examining table, I examined his lungs over his shirt, which were making an unusual sound. So, I tried to pull up his shirt to listen to his lungs without having any clothing item between my stethoscope and his skin I couldn't find the lower part of his shirt; it seemed he'd tucked into his underwear. I tried to pull the shirt up to listen to the lungs. As soon as I tried to pull up the shirt, he screamed. I asked him what was the problem? He said he was wearing overalls. I asked what were overalls? He replied that they were pants and a shirt, all in one piece that were buttoned between the thighs. I asked him to take his pants off I could examine his testicles. He took his blue jean pants off and when I looked at his underwear, I saw that it was a very tight clothing item, with the buttons between his thighs being very close to his testicles that were pulling his testicles up. I undid the buttons and loosen the lower part of the so-called overall. I asked him if he still had testicle pain. He said no. I proceeded with listening to his lungs, which were now clear. I told him that his problem seemed to be tight underwear, and the pain in the testicle was from the pressure from the overall. The shortness of breath might be a reaction to pain as his lungs were quite clear. He promised me that although he had several similar types of clothes items and wore them regularly, he would not wear them anymore.

****** 36 ******

Translation Dilemma

Although the official language in Iran is Farsi, people from different regions or religions do not speak Farsi. Patients that are illiterate are often older and may not understand Farsi if they grew up in regions where the natives speak other languages, such as Turkish, Armenian, Kurdish, Assyrian, etc., During a temporary weekend job of performing medical evaluations of the social security applicants, I experienced an interesting event. The US government usually provided and paid for interpreters if the applicant did not speak English. One day I had a patient from Iran who was Assyrian and grew up in the same region as I had, where the spoken language is Turkish. She was unable to speak Farsi but could speak in Turkish and Assyrian. The interpreter was an Armenian-Iranian woman who was able to speak English, Farsi, and Armenian but not Turkish or Assyrian. I was able to communicate with the patient but I had to translate our conversation to the government translator so she could make notes. I jokingly told her that she had to share with me the payment she would receive from the U.S. government as I had to translate the conversations to the translator!

EXPERIENCES DURING THE WORK AS A NEPHROLOGIST: 2000–2020

****** 37 ******

Devil Inside the Arm

I was asked to see a fifty-two-year-old African American minister who had been admitted to the hospital with what appeared to be kidney stones and was also in kidney failure. This patient had several other consultants treating him, including a cardiologist, a vascular surgeon, and a urologist. Upon questioning, he told me that he'd had an episode of significant pain on his left arm, along with simultaneous shaking of the left hand that was followed by a decrease in the pain but was accompanied by a significant red-black discoloration of the skin of the same extremity that lasted for several minutes. During his hospital stay, the patient had cardiac workup done, as well as ultrasound examination of the vessels of the arm to exclude possibility of any vascular event to account for his symptoms of the left arm discoloration and shaking. The kidney stones were managed by a urologist.

The cardiac workup showed no evidence of a heart problem. Upon discharge, the gentleman asked me what I thought about his arm issue. This patient was a very pleasant and funny gentleman and kept telling me that he thought that the devil went inside his arm. I jokingly told him that he might be right, and that the devil may have gone into his arm and caused an exorcist-type reaction. I said to him, "You might as well go to the church and see your Superior about it. You might get better advice from him than me." After he was discharged from the hospital, he was to be seen by a rheumatologist for possible Reynaude's phenomenon, which is secondary to some forms of connective tissue disease.

****** 38 ******

The Case of the Buried Penis

A forty-eight-year-old male weighing five-hundred-and-twenty pounds was admitted to the hospital with several co-morbidities. This patient had marked swelling of the body due to water retention, along with underlying kidney disease. He had responded to diuretic use when seen in the office, but this time he was admitted to the hospital because of exacerbation of the water retention as well as difficulty breathing and significantly abnormal blood tests that were far worse than his usual values. I was asked by the admitting hospitalist to manage the patient's fluid and electrolytes problems. The initial IV medication did not result in any urination. I was called early in the morning when the lab results became available, showing severe elevation of his blood potassium level and far worse kidney function than what it was at the time of admission. I asked the nurses to have a Foley catheter placed in on the patient and gave orders for further diuretics.

A couple of hours later I was called by nursing staff who said that they were unable to insert a Foley catheter as the patient had extreme swelling on his genital area, making it difficult to insert a Foley catheter. I advised them to have the urologist on call consulted for insertion of the Foley catheter. He couldn't insert a Foley catheter either. The penis foreskin was so swollen that it had caused backward retraction of the penis that it was impossible to visualize the tip of the penis. The urologist, who was scheduled for surgery that morning, had to leave but would come back later that morning. The urologist placed a note on the chart with the diagnosis of "a buried penis."

We had to identify the cause of his acute kidney injury to confirm that he had some urine in the bladder, so I asked for a portable kidney ultrasound and bladder scan. Because of his size and the thickness of the skin due to excessive fat and water retention, the ultrasonic waves were unable to reach the kidneys and bladder. Meanwhile, his potassium level kept rising, and his kidney function was worsening to the point where he was at risk of cardiac arrest. I asked a vascular surgeon to place a dialysis catheter in the patient so that I could give the patient temporary dialysis and remove extra potassium and fluid, but the surgeon was unable to place the catheter due to the patient's size and severe swelling of the skin; not even the longest needle was able to reach the veins on the groin or neck.

The patient's breathing worsened, and the cardiac monitor showed abnormal rhythms of the heart due to his blood's high potassium levels. The urologist returned and under local anesthesia at the bedside, he cut the foreskin—essentially performing a circumcision—and finally found the opening orifice of the penis (the urethra) and was able to insert a Foley catheter. Unfortunately, very little urine came out. I ordered a bedside injection of radiocontrast via bladder catheter to see anatomy of the bladder. Even though earlier irrigation of the catheter by urologist had not shown any urine output, suddenly with the administration of the contrast, a large volume of the urine began flowing and continued to do as we continued the course of diuretics. His potassium level improved steadily, as did his breathing and cardiac rhythms. He was alert and awake throughout the period of hospital stay. It appeared that the catheter tip had been plugged up that eventually opened after transcatheter use of radiocontrast. Over the next few days, the patient was able to improve his kidney function and reduce the swelling of his body, losing considerable amounts of weight. After several days of stay in the hospital, the patient was discharged. Upon discharge he said to me, "If this happens again, please do not resuscitate me." His established weight of over 500 pounds had been checked by himself at the zoo by animal scales because hospital scales cannot measure this kind of weight on bed scales.

A Man with Bladder and Lung Issues

I was asked to see a man in his early seventies who was admitted to the hospital with significant swelling of his body and moderate kidney failure. He had several other consultants, including cardiology, pulmonary, and urology specialists. Upon assessment by a urologist, he was found to have issues with emptying his bladder and had been advised to have intermittent catheterization of the bladder daily. His cardiologists and pulmonologists had done a workup on him and had determined that the patient was suffering from significant pulmonary hypertension, which is the elevation of the pressure inside the vessels of the lungs. As a result, the patient had been started on sildenafil (trade name Revatio), which is a lower dose of Viagra. This was to be given on a regular basis, three times a day, in an attempt to lower the pressure inside the lung vessels. This is an established treatment for pulmonary hypertension. In the case of this gentleman, any time the nurses attempted to insert the bladder catheter for urinary drainage, the patient developed an erection, preventing the nurse from inserting the catheter, which embarrassed both the nurse and the patient. Eventually, a decision was made to place a Foley catheter for continuous drainage while in the hospital, along with using diuretics to eliminate the extra water that the patient had retaining. Several days later, the patient was discharged home after having been trained for self-catheterization and was advised to continue taking the sildenafil. His renal function improved with use of continuous urine drainage and diuretics.

A Confused CNA

During one of my hospital rounds, I entered the room of a patient who had end-stage kidney disease and was on chronic dialysis. I noted that the certified nursing assistant (CNA) was checking the patient's blood pressure on his left arm. I knew that the patient had dialysis-access arteriovenous fistula on that arm and should not have been subjected to blood-pressure checks or have blood samples drawn from that arm to maintain patency of the shunt. I asked the CNA to stop what she was doing and pointed to the sign on the wall saying, "Don't you see that sign that says no blood drawing or blood pressure check on the left arm?" She replied yes, she had seen that sign, but she was checking the right arm. I repeated that this was the patient's left arm that she was performing that blood pressure check on, not the right. She said, "Wait." She asked the patient to move to the other side of the bed and then she laid down next to him to see whether the arm that the patient had his shunt inserted was on the left side or right. She then admitted she was wrong and apologized. I had to explain to her that when one faces a patient, your right is his left and your left is his right side, and then I joked, "By the way, this also applies to female patients as well." She apologized again and removed the blood pressure cuff from the left arm and placed it on the right arm of the patient.

The Case of the Texas Catheter

A sixty-six-year-old male had coronary artery bypass graft surgery done, but unfortunately, he had a cardiac arrest intraoperatively. He'd been successfully resuscitated after a period of cardiac standstill. He eventually completed the procedure and was transferred to the ICU for post-operative care. Due to prolonged periods of low blood pressure and compromised blood flow to the vital organs during his cardiac arrest, we were expecting some degree of multisystem injuries. He remained comatose and developed kidney failure requiring daily dialysis. His comatose state lasted several days during which he was not making any urine; because of the risk of infection through the bladder catheter, we'd had to remove the catheter. Eventually he woke up, and to our surprise was able to respond to questions appropriately. He stayed on dialysis for several weeks.

He was eventually transferred out of ICU. By then he was coherent and talkative, and he told me, "Doc, I think I am making urine." In those days, we did not have a bladder scan to measure urine volume within the bladder, and when I asked the nurse, she confirmed he was wetting the diaper slightly. So, I asked the nurse to insert a Texas catheter on him and measure the volume of his urine over a twenty-four-hour period. A Texas catheter is essentially a condom with a tube connected to its tip where the urine can be drained in the bag on an incontinent patient to measure the volume of the urine that the patient is putting out.

On the next day when I made my rounds, I noticed that the twenty-four-hour urine output had not been recorded on the patient's chart. I became upset and asked where was the nurse who was taking care of the patient yesterday? The same nurse who was looking after the patient the prior day was also taking care of him that day. I admit I was angry and asked her, "Didn't I ask for placement of the Texas catheter on this patient yesterday?" She looked at me and replied, "Yes, you did." I then told her that I had just checked the patient, he did not have a catheter, and she had not charted his urine volume over the last twenty-four hours. She was a very shy person, she looked at me and stammered," But... but..." Then she showed her index finger and her thumb only slightly apart, and said in a very quiet voice, "But he's too small and the catheter wouldn't stay in." I got the message and immediately apologized for raising my voice. She was right. The patient's genital was quite small and unable to keep the catheter in as the condom kept "popping out." Blood tests over the next few days showed improvement of the kidney function without interim dialysis to the point that we were able to stop dialysis and was subsequently transferred the patient to a rehab unit.

****** 42 ******

How Do You Feel?

A seventy-two-year-old married man, who regularly attended a dancing class twice a week with his wife, finished two consecutive fast dances with different partners followed by a slow dance with his wife of fifty-five years. Shortly after starting the dance to the tune of *You Light Up My Life*, he collapsed and became unconscious. Someone in attendance immediately started CPR and they called paramedics. Paramedics arrived a few minutes later and noted that the patient had had a cardiac arrest. They defibrillated the patient and were able to resume his cardiac rhythm but lost it again. They resumed CPR during his transfer to the emergency room. Upon his arrival, he was noted to be in ventricular fibrillation and cardiac arrest. He was defibrillated again, intubated, and placed on a ventilator; they were now able to detect a pulse and blood pressure.

He was transferred to ICU where he was noted to have no urine output, so we, the kidney specialists, were consulted. According to his wife, this patient had had no history of health problems. He rapidly improved, and on the following day he was extubated. When I arrived to visit him, the patient's wife, who was at his bedside, told me patient was unresponsive. I screamed very loudly, "Mr. B., do you hear me?" He mumbled something, and his wife became very excited. Then I said, "Mr. B., how do you feel?" To my surprise, he responded immediately, saying "With my hand." At this point, his wife jumped up screaming, "Hallelujah! he is back!"

Later he joked, "I was dancing with my wife to *You Light Up My Life* when all the lights went out on me!" The patient recovered fully and was discharged home the following week.

******* 43 *******

Pulse Oximetry

When a patient in the psychiatric ward began getting short of breath, the nurse asked the ward clerk to call the patient's primary doctor, who did so. However, when the doctor called back, the clerk was unable to locate the nurse to give the report. This doctor had a foreign accent. He asked ward clerk what was the issue? The clerk said that the patient was having some difficulty breathing. This doctor, who did not want to wait for the nurse to return, said, "Okay, why don't you fill out a form and ask the respiratory department to do a pulse ox and call me with the results." Given his accent, it sounded like he was saying "pool ox" instead of pulse ox. The ward clerk asked again, "What do you want, Doctor? What should I write on the form?" The doctor repeated his orders and hung up. The ward clerk filled the requisition, stating that the doctor asked for "pool socks." Upon receiving the request, the respiratory tech made multiple photocopies of the form and sent it to all the nursing stations. This poor ward clerk became an object of jokes and teasing to the point he resigned.

****** 44 ******

An Accidental Occurrence Helping to Diagnose a Condition

I was asked to see a patient who was a young man in his thirties who had been beaten up on the street and had been brought in by police after having suffered severe physical trauma. The patient had been intubated and admitted to the ICU. During the preliminary exam. he was found to have abnormal kidney function, which is why I had been consulted. This patient, who had been quite healthy and athletic before he was assaulted, was now unable to move his lower extremities and was feverish and had difficulty breathing. The patient had been awake and was receiving mild sedation to keep him comfortable while on the ventilator. When I entered the ICU to visit him, I noticed that the curtain on the patient's room had been pulled closed. I asked the staff what was going on, and they said that the patient was being cleaned up, and that a neurologist was there also waiting to assess the patient.

    I began to discuss the case with the neurologist, who told me that based on the fever, the paralysis in the lower limbs, and his difficulty breathing, a diagnosis of Guillain-Barre syndrome was possible as was a spinal cord injury due to trauma and transverse myelitis. While we were waiting for opportunity to assess the patient, a female nurse wearing a gown and mask pulled open the curtain and asked one of the male nurses to help her.

    A few minutes later the curtain was pulled back. The female nurse was blushing and acting nervous. We asked her what happened? She explained that as she was cleaning this patient's stomach and genitals, he had developed this enormous erection, which is why she called the male nurse to assist her. The neurologist looked at me and said, "Well, I don't have to do a lumbar puncture now." The presence of the erection meant he didn't have a spinal cord injury. I went in to do my evaluation of potential causes of his kidney issues. If the nurse hadn't been cleaning him and observed his erection, the neurologist could have been obligated to do an unnecessary lumbar puncture on this man.

****** 45 ******

Newly Diagnosed Diabetic Man Complaining of His Diet

I had a patient whom I had been treating for over three years for high blood pressure and moderate kidney dysfunction. The gentleman was a Middle Eastern man who frequently came with his wife and daughter. One day following a screening lab test, I noted that he had elevated blood sugar and a high amount of sugar in his urine. He was not known to have diabetes before, and screening labs of previous year had shown a normal blood sugar level. I rechecked his urine in the office to verify the lab report; his urine had a significant amount of the sugar in it. I told him that he appeared to be diabetic. He asked me, "What is diabetes?" I had to explain to him that it is elevation of sugar in the blood. He told me that he didn't have sugar in his blood. I said, "Everyone has sugar in the blood, but yours is too high." I told him that he had to follow a certain diet, and I gave him prescription for a pill for him to take to regulate his sugar level. I scheduled him for a follow-up appointment in six weeks and that he was going to have to repeat the lab tests.

On his next appointment, he came with his wife and daughter per the usual. I asked him how he was doing? He replied not so well. Hmmm. I asked, "Why not?" He said, "You see these two women?" He pointed at his wife and daughter. I said yes. He said that they had accompanied him on his last visit, right? I said, "Yes, they did." He said, "We went home from the office after my visit, and what do you think I had for dinner that day?" I said I didn't know. He said chicken. Then he said, "What do you think I had for breakfast the following day?" I said I didn't know. He said, "Chicken. And what do you think I had for lunch that day?" I said I didn't know. He said, "Chicken. What do you think I have been having for all meals since then?" I said, "I presume it was mostly chicken." He said, "You're absolutely right. Doctor, I have eaten so much chicken that nowadays anytime I hear the crowing of a rooster, I bend forward." Both wife and daughter began to blush and were literally speechless. I was laughing myself sick.

****** 46 ******

Sending Kisses while on a Breathing Machine

An Iranian man in his sixties had heart surgery for the second time for a redo of his coronary artery bypass graft surgery. He had a very caring and rather well-informed wife. During surgery, he developed significant issues, but it was eventually successful, and the patient was brought to the ICU following the surgery. His cardiac surgeon was in the ICU post-surgery when the patient's heart suddenly stopped. A code blue was called, and a resuscitating team rushed to the patient. Given that his chest had been opened to perform the bypass procedure, doing ordinary cardiopulmonary resuscitation via chest compressions would have been very risky and less effective. The surgeon immediately asked for a sterile gown and glove. At the patient's bedside in the ICU, he opened the patient's chest from the suture sites he'd stitched that same day, spread incision site wide, and thrust his hand into patient's chest and began to manually massage this man's heart.

After a while, the cardiac monitor showed that the heart had begun working again. When asked to check his blood pressure, the nurses were able to determine the presence of a blood pressure along with a palpable pulse. The patient was taken back to the operating room, but the manual massage had caused so much swelling that the surgeon was unable to close the chest because of the enlargement of the heart and the tissue around it. To close the chest to prevent infection, an exterior piece of plastic was placed in between the edges of two incisions, leaving a gap of nearly a couple of inches. One could easily see this man's heart beating through this plastic.

I was consulted to treat this patient for acute injury to his kidneys, which had occurred due to his cardiac arrest. He was diabetic as well, but overall, from a kidney standpoint, he'd been in reasonable shape. This patient was intubated and placed on a ventilator for several days. After a day or two, his level of sedation was reduced, and he was able to comprehend speech. He was advised that he was sedated and should not try to fight back the tube on his throat. His hands were tied to ensure that he wouldn't pull out his breathing tube from his mouth. Although he was unable to understand English, I was able to communicate with him in Farsi.

During my visits when he was alert and awake, he was always smiling. I observed his heart beating vigorously through the plastic patch. While I was attending him and talking to him, his heart surgeon walked in. I told the patient, "This is your heart surgeon." The patient was looking at the surgeon with tears in his eyes. Suddenly, he wrapped his lips around his endotracheal tube connected to breathing machine and sent the surgeon kisses over and over by opening his mouth around the tube and then closing again, pretending that he was sending kisses. The surgeon in return sent a kiss back to him.

This was one of the memorable moments of my practice that I will never forget. Looking at the patient's chest, seeing his heart beating like crazy while at the same time looking at the patient's face and seeing him smile, then cry, and then send kisses. The patient was able to be discharged from the hospital after the swelling of his heart reduced. They removed the plastic and closed his chest wall. His wife was able to keep him alive and active for several years. I treated him as an outpatient in my office for years for his chronic kidney disease and diabetes. He always said that he owed his life to his wife and his heart surgeon.

****** 47 ******

Damn Iverson

In 2001 Los Angeles Lakers had reached the finals of the NBA playoffs. Shaquille O'Neal and Kobe Bryant were the stars of the Lakers. The final series of the playoffs was between the Los

Angeles Lakers and the Philadelphia 76ers. The first game, which was played in Los Angeles, was won by Philadelphia, taking away the home court advantage from the Lakers. On the day of the second game, which also was being played at Los Angeles, I was on call and had to make rounds in different hospitals. Every time I'd stop in one of my patient's rooms, I'd watch the TV with them to see where the score is. As our group covered patients in different hospitals, I'd listen to the radio to see how the game was going while driving to the other hospital. Once I arrived at the second hospital, I was curious to find out what the score was, as it had taken me some time to get from my car to the ward where I had to make my rounds.

The first patient I saw was an Armenian gentleman who had no interest in basketball and was not watching the game. I interviewed and examined him and went back to the nursing station to chart his condition. Meanwhile, quite a bit of time had elapsed, and I was getting very anxious about the score as this was the second game. If the Lakers lost this game at home for the second time in a row, their chances of coming back and beating the 76ers on the best of seven games would be quite low.

My next patient was also an Armenian lady who was watching an Armenian program. I saw her, then left her room to go to the nursing station for charting, but on my way to the nursing station, I heard the noise of spectators from a room as I was walking by. The patient inside that room was not mine. As I was desperate to find out the score, I eased my way into the room to peek at the TV for the score. Although the game was ongoing, but the TV screen at that time was not showing the score as players kept missing the basket, and in absence of a score change, it was not being shown. I quickly looked at the patient who was an old lady sitting on the chair but either sleeping or unresponsive. Meanwhile, I tried to watch the game and still there was no score showing on the screen. I watched the lady again, who appeared to be asleep, but I didn't notice her breathing. I was getting very nervous, both for not knowing the score and afraid that this woman had died in her chair. Since she was not my patient, and I was the last person in her room, I could have been blamed for some wrongdoing.

I decided to rush back to the nursing station and let the nurses know about this patient. But before I did, I had a last look at the TV still showing no score. I turned around to exit the room and return to the nursing station. Suddenly I heard a loud female voice say, "Sit down, what's the score?" I turned around, and sure enough it was the patient who was asking me about the score. She was alive and coherent! I introduced myself, explaining that although she was not my patient, the TV in the room of my patient next door was on a different channel. Upon hearing the roar of crowd coming from her room, I'd slipped into her room. She then asked me again, "OK, what's the score?" I told her I didn't know, but at that very moment, Iverson scored and when the cameras moved to the scoreboard, it showed that the Lakers were behind. She screamed, "That damn Iverson." I sat next to her and we chatted and watched the game until halftime, when I had to leave to see my other patients. That game was won at the last second by the Lakers, and the series won by the Lakers in the seventh game.

48 ******

What Is Up?

An Armenian woman in her fifties who did not speak English was admitted to the hospital with acute kidney injury superimposed on severe chronic kidney diseases, in addition to suffering from psychosis. She was an office patient of mine and was approaching dialysis dependency prior to this admission. The placing of a dialysis catheter and shunt (arterio-venous fistula) was performed. Following surgery, she complained of pain and anxiety and was given Vicodin for pain and Ativan for anxiety. Immediately after this she was fed by her daughter. The patient then vomited and aspirated the vomitus, developing respiratory arrest and had to be intubated and placed on a ventilator. She was unresponsive for about thirty-six hours even though no further sedation had been given. Then she opened her eyes but was not following commands. She was extubated but continued to remain unresponsive to any question or commands when given in her own language either by us or her family. But according to the nurses she appeared to be, at times, following commands. When I arrived to visit her the following day, the daughter who was also in the room, stated that her mother was unresponsive. The patient who knew me from previous visits, had opened her eyes when I entered the room and looked at me. She suddenly screamed, "What's up!" Her daughter was ecstatic saying, "She's back!" That was the only phrase she knew in English, which she had learned from her grandchild.

****** 49 ******

Doc, Don't Bother Me, I'm Busy

A very pleasant Latino male in his sixties who had very severe cardiomyopathy and heart-failure was in the ICU. He had expressed his desire not to have intubation or cardiac resuscitation in event of any mishap. In addition to heart problems, he was diabetic with kidney involvement and cirrhosis of the liver, along with the breathing problem related to his heart failure. He had low blood pressure and was receiving medications for his condition., Such medications can only be administered in the ICU. He also was on multiple other medications for his other medical problems.

When I entered his room as I made my rounds, I saw that there are three very beautiful women surrounding the patient spoon feeding him homemade food. The man, who always joked with me in the past, looked at me and said, "Hey, doc, don't bother me today. Can't you see I am busy?" Everybody laughed and I left the room saying in an imitation of Arnold Schwarzenegger, "I shall be back." I did go back to his room later, and by that time the ladies had left. We had always teased each other a lot, and he always had a funny comeback for me. Unfortunately, the patient did not make it out of the hospital and died few days later. I still remember that he never lost his sense of humor even given how extremely ill he was.

****** 50 ******

Cheating Pacemaker

An African American woman in her seventies was seen in consultation for kidney problems. The main reason for her hospital admission was an infection on her pacemaker wire. She had had a pacemaker inserted many years ago, and the work-up for her fever revealed she had a fungus ball or vegetation full of infection on the tip of the pacemaker inside her heart, which had been detected by echocardiogram. It was decided to remove the pacemaker but because the infection was inside the heart and most likely the germs were circulating with the blood, the new pacemaker could not be placed in at the same time the other pacemaker was being removed due to risk of having the second pacemaker become infected as well. She had to have an external pacemaker for a while until the blood infection had completely cleared and then have another pacemaker inserted. She asked me why we couldn't immediately install a second pacemaker. She had been extremely serious the entire time I was treating her. I apprised her of these complications, and because she was so serious and anxious, I added, "Due to infection of the initial pacemaker, she had to divorce the first pacemaker because the pacemaker had cheated on her and had developed an STD, so he deserved to be divorced." Again, in a joking manner, I advised she should warn her second partner against cheating, in other words, her second pacemaker was her next partner. Finally, she smiled.

****** 51 ******

Doctor, Are You Married?

An Armenian woman in her eighties had been admitted to the hospital with septic shock and a severe infection with sustained low blood pressure, acute kidney injury, and multi-organ failure. My partner, who happens to be a very handsome young man, was talking to the family at the family meeting. As the patient was intubated and was unconscious, he explained her medical status and required the family to decide on her code status. Many of her family members had come to the hospital, and my partner wanted to know if the patient had mentioned anything to the family members in the past regarding her wishes on resuscitation, dialysis, or other artificial means of keeping her alive. Based on her numerous issues, multisystem failure, low blood pressure, and old age, my partner told the family that any chance of meaningful survival and the likelihood of her returning to preadmission status was near zero. After explaining all this, he asked the family if they had any questions. The granddaughter of the patient, who happened to be in her early twenties, raised her hand. When my partner asked her what was her question? She said, "Doctor, are you married?" He didn't know how to answer that, while all the other family members began laughing.

****** 52 ******

Doctor, Can You Come a Little Later?

In January of 2011, I was asked to see a pregnant woman on the labor and delivery floor, who was experiencing high-blood pressure and protein in her urine. This condition of pregnancy is called preeclampsia, but similar problems can occur in pregnant women with pre-existing kidney problems that were not diagnosed prior to pregnancy. When I entered her hospital room, she was watching a football game on the television. When I introduced myself and explained the reason why I was there, she said to me, "Doctor, I'm sorry there's only fifty-three seconds left in this game Can I watch the end of the game before we talk about my kidney problems?" She continued by saying that the game was between New York Jets and Indianapolis Colts, and she had a crush on the quarterback of the Jets, "Mark Sanchez." It was a very close game, and the Jets were on the verge of winning. She asked me if I could wait a few minutes until the game was over. I said "Sure," and went to the nursing station to review her chart. When I returned to interview her after the game, she was a happy camper as the Jets had beat the Colts 17 to 16 even though the great Peyton Manning was the Colts' quarterback. She had more interest in talking about football with me than her own medical problem.

53 ******

Interrogation by a Woman Who Was a CIA Agent

A gentleman in his sixties was running on a treadmill when he collapsed. His wife told me that both were "Federal Agents." She was a very pleasant Latina woman who found the husband on the floor next to the treadmill having jerky movements. He was unresponsive. She started CPR and called the paramedics, who brought the patient to the hospital and who was subsequently resuscitated. He had been transferred to the ICU by the time I saw him. The patient was unconscious and continued to have jerky movements of the body related to the poor oxygenation of the brain and the damage to the brain during the event. His wife told me from the sounds of it that she didn't think that her husband would regain consciousness and return to his pre-existing status. I concurred with her.

I noted that based on her job-related experiences she kept her cool and sense of humor to the point that she asked me where I was from. I jokingly said, "Nicaragua." She said, "Really" With that last name?" and then she started talking to me in Spanish. I said, "I'm sorry, I have a hearing problem." and she smiled. Then I said, "Listen, I'm not under any oath to answer your questions correctly, am I?" She smiled again. I then told her my history as a doctor and discussed with her the husband's code status. We subsequently did an electroencephalogram (EEG), which revealed extensive damage to the brain. She brought us a copy of the husband's advanced directive. Based on the wife's request and in keeping with the patient's previously documented directive, we placed the patient on what is known as "comfort care."

****** 54 ******

The Patient I Couldn't Remember

One interesting event occurred was when a homeless man was brought into the hospital suffering from a drug overdose and kidney failure. This man, who was in his forties when he was admitted to the ICU and I first examined him, had long hair and a beard. The following day, when I came to make the rounds, I looked around for my patient, double checked that the room number was correct but was sure that the patient in that room was not the same one I'd seen the previous day. However, the patient had had a severe infestation of lice on his scalp and beard when he was admitted, and the nurse had shaved his beard and cut hair, making a new man out of him. The patient was grateful for the shave and haircut and thanked the nurse.

****** 55 ******

The Story of My Workaholic Cardiologist Colleague

An extremely hard-working and dedicated cardiologist was a friend and colleague of mine. In his early seventies he had been admitted to the ICU as a patient to undergo heart catheterization for a work-up of angina. All his professional life he came to the hospital before 6 am and left the hospital after 6 pm. Even though he was at retirement age and financially secure, he had continued to work. His heart catheterization had been scheduled for 11 am that day. I asked the nurses where he was, and the nurses told me that he was making rounds on his own patients. I caught up with him and noticed that he was still wearing the hospital gown issued to all patients; he was examining patients wearing the same gown they were wearing. I laughingly asked him if he were going to bill his patients' insurance for these visits while his cardiologist will bill his insurance for the same-day cardiac catheterization?

He underwent his cardiac catheterization and following the catheterization he was brought back to the ICU. While in the ICU, he began complaining of numbness and tingling sensation in his feet. Question of possible microemboli—meaning that the small clots of the blood were migrating to his feet during the catheterization procedure—was considered. The other concern were possible problems related to his well-known lower-back issues, which could have been aggravated by his lying down on the bed for too long.

His primary physician arrived and began to massage his feet in the hopes of improving his discomfort. I left the room to see my other patients. About half an hour later I returned to my cardiologist friend's room and noticed that his primary doctor was still massaging his feet. I asked him if he was any better and he said no. I said okay I'll come back later. I left the room and noted that one of our nurses who is originally from Thailand was on duty taking care of another patient in ICU. I told her that what I want you to do is to go back to my cardiologist friend's room and tell him that the massage wasn't working is because he is being given a Swedish massage and that is why it is not working. Tell him that you can give him a Thai massage to see if that helps. His primary doctor laughed, but my cardiologist friend did not.

Three days later my cardiologist friend was back at work. I asked him how his feet were, and he said they are OK. Then he looked at me and said, "What was that issue with that massage?" Suddenly he started laughing. When he finished laughing, he said, "Now I understand what you were trying to say in relation to different kinds of massage. So, your comment on trying to switch from Swedish massage to a Thai massage was a joke." I said, "You need to rest a little more to improve your reflexes. This is too late for reaction by a smart and sharp man. I hope having a heart catheter didn't affect your brilliant and sharp mind." He laughed and said, "Those were the days."

****** 56 ******

Kicking Marks

An Armenian-speaking gentleman in his late sixties with a history of heart problems was admitted to the ICU. He spoke no English. I was treating him for his kidney issues. One day when I went to see him, I was told that he'd been transferred out of ICU to a telemetry unit. I went to the telemetry unit and, fortunately, his daughter was there, who was quite fluent in English. After examining him and explaining the status of the kidney function, which had been temporarily damaged by angiography dye that he had received earlier, I told him he was recovering. At that moment I asked him through his daughter if he had any questions. When the daughter translated my question, the daughter told me that the father wanted to know why he was transferred out of ICU. I responded that his health had improved enough that he had "graduated" from the ICU. I jokingly said that they kicked him out of ICU, and, as a matter of, fact I wanted to see if he had any bruises on the side of his butt where he was kicked. Obviously, I was joking. The daughter laughed and translated what I said to her father. The father stood up and brought his hand to his hip, at which time the daughter started laughing louder. Then in Armenian she said something to her father, who took his hands off his hip and laughed as well. The daughter stated that the father took me at my word and was going to pull down his pants to check for bruises on his butt, she stopped by telling him I was only joking.

****** 57 ******

Issues of a Woman

I was consulted on a very pleasant and active ninety-three-year-old Caucasian female who had been admitted with low serum sodium level. When I interviewed her, she told me she was having multiple issues and was wondering whether her low sodium count had anything to do with it. When I asked what her issues were, she said that she could no longer bowl as well as she used to, even though she was still competing in a bowling league. She asked my advice about resigning from her team, concerned that it wasn't fair to the other team members. She also said that she was lonely, and that she, "Couldn't find anybody my age. My best friend is twenty years younger than me." She stated that she still lived by herself at home and wondered whether she should move to a board and care or assisted living place. I told her that at her age, people usually were living in assisted living or board and care places. Why was she still living alone? She said because she can handle it, she liked not being dependent on anybody, and that she was the manager of the apartment building that she owned and lived in.

She then asked me if I wanted her to mow my lawn. I said no thank you because child labor was illegal in this country. She laughed. I sat down with her in her room and had a long conversation about her issues as well as about politics and life. Her low sodium of the blood was medication-induced and by stopping medication she improved and subsequently discharged home, although she'd decided to move into an assisted living facility.

****** 58 ******

The Lady with the Mysterious Touch

I was consulted on an eighty-seven-year-old Iranian Armenian woman for electrolyte problems. During the interview she said, "Doctor, any man who I touch ends up dying." She was curious whether this has anything to do with her electrolyte abnormalities. When I asked her for further explanation, she stated that her husband died recently. Her primary doctor died shortly after her husband from a car accident, and her gastroenterologist, who had performed a colonoscopy on her just a couple of months earlier, had also died. I jokingly told her that I may call another kidney doctor to see her now because I didn't want to touch her. She began laughing.

****** 59 ******

The Story of the Nurse Who Liked to Talk

I was involved in treating a dialysis-dependent woman who was in ICU because of an infection due to the dialysis catheter. She had developed sepsis—widespread infection of the body— and had very low blood pressure, which required intubation and mechanical ventilation to help her breathe. She had been placed in chemically induced coma. A few days after admission, her vital signs improved and subsequently she woke up. She had been extubated and was alert and coherent. In the morning when I went to see the patient for the first time after her extubation. I was introduced to her by her bedside nurse for that day. The nurse told the patient that I was the kidney doctor who had been looking after her during her hospital stay. The nurse who had a habit of talking a lot, continued to talk with the patient while I was waiting to speak to the patient. The patient clearly wanted to ask some questions but kept listening politely to this nurse, who seemingly had no intention of stopping her chatter.

I finally had to interrupt her and tell her to stop talking. Then I told the patient that she may want to ask me some questions, and please know this nurse of hers is a very good nurse except for the fact that she exercises her tongue too much. I told the patient that I had some unused ear plugs in my car because I am sensitive to wind in my ears, and I'd be happy to bring her a pair so she could insert them for today until this nurse's shift was over. We all laughed.

****** 60 ******

He's the One Who Stole My Panties

An older woman with dementia had been admitted to a regular surgical ward to undergo surgery for vulvar cancer. Her room was very close to the nursing station. I had never seen this patient nor was I involved in her care. The nursing station on this ward is in front of the elevator doors. I had just come out of the elevator to see some of my patients when this woman, who was standing in the doorway of her room, suddenly began pointing her finger at me, saying something in Armenian that I did not understand. Three of the nurses at the station were of Armenian ethnicity and understood what she was saying. All three began laughing loud, and no matter how many times I questioned them, they couldn't stop laughing. Finally, one of them managed to stop laughing and told me that she had accused me of stealing her underwear. All the nurses began laughing then. From then on, a couple of these nurses would jokingly cross their arms and hands in front of their hips whenever they saw me, saying, "Here comes the panty stealer!"

****** 61 ******

Sign of a Stroke in a Forty-Year-Old Woman

I was asked to see a forty-year-old woman who had been admitted to the hospital with pneumonia. She had had a kidney transplant several years ago, and I had been asked to oversee her transplant medication regimen and watch her kidney function during her hospital stay. When I asked about her past medical history, she mentioned that she had high blood pressure for a long time, which caused her kidney failure. Initially she went on dialysis but subsequently needed a kidney transplant. When I asked if she had other medical conditions I should know about, she said she'd had stroke. When I asked her to tell me her symptoms—as I was doubtful that a forty-year-old woman would have had a history of strokes in the past—she said that she had uncontrollable winking with her left eye all day. I said, "But winking alone does not mean that you're having a stroke. As a matter of fact, I do it whenever I see a pretty woman. Did you see a handsome young man that day?" She laughed. It is likely that she had some electrolyte imbalance, which is not unusual in transplanted patients, although some neurological condition could have accounted for that as well but not a stroke.

****** 62 ******

My Blood Pressure Is Not the Only Thing That Goes Up

An eighty-four-year-old Armenian clergyman had been admitted with a kidney problem and high blood pressure. He was on the medical floor in a private room. One morning when I entered the room, a very young nurse was checking his blood pressure. As soon as she saw me, she yelled at me saying that his blood pressure was 190 over 95. I then told the patient that when a pretty nurse was checking one's blood pressure, it was going to go up. He replied, "Yes, doc, the blood pressure is not the only thing that goes up when pretty girls check it." The nurse blushed and told me that now she needed to go to church; we all laughed.

****** 63 ******

Let Me Call Doctor L.

I was asked to see an Arab Armenian lady with kidney problems. When I entered the exam room, her husband was present. I them that I was a kidney doctor, and I had been asked to see her. The patient asked, "Are you Doctor L.?" I replied, "No, but if you want, I can assign Dr. L to see you instead." She said, "No, no, Doctor. We knew a family in Beirut with that last name, and we keep hearing that name being paged on overhead speakers. We thought it might be you." I told them that my name was Dr Farboody, but that Dr L. was also a kidney doctor but not with my group, and that I had no problem calling him to see her if she preferred. They both said no, that if their primary doctor had referred her to me, they'd prefer to be seen by me.

I then asked her about her medical history. She removed three pieces of paper from her handbag and began reading: vasculitis, inflammatory bowel disease, entero vaginal fistula, sarcoidosis, and chronic kidney disease. At this point I said, "Okay, why don't you give me those papers so I can make a copy of them, and I'll give the original back to you." I then asked what medications she'd been on? She pulled out another three pieces of paper and started to read. I held up a hand to stop her from reading any more. "Hold on and let me call Dr. L.to treat you." Both she and husband started laughing. This woman became my outpatient whom I treated for several years. One of the funniest statements her husband made during one of their visits was in 2015 when he said, "Doctor, would you tell her to agree to go for a vacation because last time that we took a vacation Ronald Reagan was president."

64 ******

Put the Mask Back On

A funny Filipina nurse whom I used to tease a lot was sitting behind the computer taking a competency test. As she had refused to receive the flu vaccine, she had to wear a mask during her shift as it was mandatory. She was wearing a mask and sitting behind the computer when I arrived. She stood up to greet me. I told her that I hadn't seen her for a long time as she had been on vacation. She replied that she had gone to the Philippines. Then I said, "You look really good." She pulled down her mask and replied, "Thanks, Doctor Farb. That's very nice of you." I told her to put the mask back on, that she looked better that way. She laughed and told me that I was awful.

65 ******

The Monitor Technician Who Was Feeling Cold

A monitor technician I worked with was in her late fifties. One day she kept saying that she was very cold and kept asking everybody if they were cold as well. Because everyone she asked replied that they weren't cold, she became worried. She kept repeating that she didn't know why she was so cold that day. Suddenly she said, "I know now why I'm cold! I forgot to put on my bra today." Everybody began laughing. It was late November when this happened. Just as a joke, I asked my daughter to buy a red bra from Victoria Secret for her so I could give it to her as a Christmas gift. After New Year's when I saw her, she stated that it fit her perfectly; however, she refused to provide any proof.

****** 66 ******

Invention of a Homeless Man on Holding His Urine

A sixty-year-old man, with a history of multiple substance abuse and bouts of homelessness, had developed multiple electrolyte abnormalities and kidney problems, all related to his substance abuse. I was asked to see him regarding these issues. Upon further questioning, he stated that he no longer could hold his urine when he felt the urge to urinate. Since he was homeless, sometimes he wet his pants, but he had recently found a solution for this incontinence. I asked him, "What is your solution?" He replied that since he was not circumcised, when he got the urge to go and there was no bathroom available, he immediately pulled the foreskin of his penis forward, blocking the hole on the tip and then pees a little. He'd then look for a bathroom and when found one, he'd remove his hand off and relieve himself. I told him that this was probably one of the advantages of not having been circumcised and he laughed.

****** 67 ******

Am I In the Philippines?

A gentleman in his late sixties who had a Filipina lady as caregiver had been having an endoscopy of the stomach and colon. Once admitted to the GI unit, he was given medication to put him to sleep—what we call conscious sedation—and an endoscope was inserted for the colonoscopy. Suddenly, his heart rhythm went chaotic and his blood pressure dropped, so the gastroenterologist had to pull out the endoscope and terminate the procedure. His rhythm improved upon withdrawal of the endoscope, and the patient was immediately sent to the intensive care unit for observation and management of the heart rhythm. The patient's caregiver accompanied the patient to the ICU. The patient was still sedated and unable to communicate. The patient was promptly placed in an ICU bed. I was monitoring him from the monitoring station when his heart rhythm went chaotic again and the monitor alarm began shrieking. The monitor technician screamed that the patient in Room 10 was in ventricular tachycardia; all the nurses rushed to the bedside to initiate cardiopulmonary resuscitation. At this moment, his cardiac rhythm returned spontaneously to a regular rhythm. Soon after he opened his eyes, looked around, and then suddenly screamed, "Am I in the Philippines?" All the nurses that day were of Filipino descent Everybody laughed and told him that, no, he was still in the United States. His cardiac issue is called Torsade De Pointes, which is medication-induced ventricular tachycardia. His cardiologist changed some of his medications and he did not have any further problems.

What Form of Anxiety?

One evening when I had finished my rounds in the hospital, I was waiting for the elevator so I could go home. This hospital had six elevators, with each elevator having a large capacity for several people. The elevators were quite slow as it was the time of night when the nursing staff usually changed shifts. Finally, one of the elevators stopped and the door opened, but the elevator was packed with nurses trying to leave their shift. I told them it was okay, that I'd wait for the next elevator. They beckoned me in and tried to move back to give me enough room. I squeezed in and faced the elevator door. The door closed, almost hitting my nose we were packed in so tightly. Somebody from the back said, "Doctor, did you notice that everybody here is a woman and you're the only man?" I did not respond. Then another person from the back said, "Don't you wish you had all these women in your bedroom?" Again, I did not respond. Then the same woman said, "Hey Doc, are we giving you anxiety?" By this time, the elevator had reached the ground floor, but I had to say something. Then I responded, "Yes, it is giving me anxiety, but do you know what type of anxiety?" She said no. I said, "Performance anxiety." They all broke out laughing. At that point, the elevator door opened and a bunch of nurses waiting for the elevators saw all of us laughing and asked what was going on. I just ran away. The next day a few people jokingly asked me how was my night last night? Was I anxious?

****** 69 ******

A Language Barrier of a Foreign-Born Nurse

Early one morning I was asked to consult on a young man who was in the emergency room, who had been brought in by the police from the jail for profound weakness. The emergency room physician had done some lab tests and had found out that the patient had an abnormal kidney function test. I was called in to see if I could determine the cause of his kidney failure. The patient, who was a tall muscular man, stated that previously he had been very healthy man. I asked the lab to do a stat (meaning immediate) blood test for a muscle enzyme called CK. After placing the orders for intravenous fluid along with some other medications and above lab tests, I left the emergency room to check on my in-patients. That was about 10 a.m. I was done by noon, after which I left that hospital to see my patients at another hospital. My rounds were done by 6 pm, and I was thankful that I wasn't scheduled for the office that day.

Subsequently, I forgot about this case until 11 p.m. that night when the exchange service phoned me as I was on call that night for the group. They told me that the hospital had called, and they needed to put me through to them. The nurse who answered the phone had a pronounced accent. She said, "I have this patient that you saw this morning." I responded yes. She said, "I have the lab results for you." I said, "What lab results?" She said, "The CK results." Then I remembered. I had forgotten to follow up on these lab results. But I had asked for the results stat. I reminded her, "I asked for these results stat and you are calling me now with the results? What are they?" She apologized but said that they had just received them. I asked her for the results. "She said, "I don't know." I had just woken up from a deep sleep for a lab result that she couldn't tell me the results. "What do you mean you don't know?" I was quite annoyed. She said, "Okay, this is the result: two, three, six, seven, nine, four. What is this DOKTOR?" I asked, "Is this the test result of the test?" She said yes. I asked her to tell me what the name of the test was. She said, "CK." I asked her to read me the results again. She repeated the previous numbers again, reading one digit at a time. Then I realized that she was unable to read the exact English version of the same number which would be 236,794; because of the language barrier, she was unable to do it in English. I asked for the lab results to be repeated in the morning and change the intravenous medication. The upper limit of normal range for CK is about 200. The morning repeat test results were very close to the ones reported the previous night.

The following morning, I went to see the patient. He was being guarded by an officer from the jail. I asked the officer to stand outside in the corridor for a few minutes so I could talk to the patient in private. Then I asked the patient what happened. Two days earlier he was arrested and taken to jail. While in jail, he was forced to do push-ups until he collapsed. The following day, he had such profound trauma to his muscles that he was unable to walk and had to be brought to the emergency room after promising the officers that he would keep his mouth shut. He asked me not to report that he'd been forced to do all those push-up issues. I told him that I was obligated by law to refer this issue to the social services for follow up. His kidney failure was related to elevation of these particular muscle enzymes due to strenuous exercise. Within a few days of being hydrated, his numbers improved. He was subsequently discharged with the primary service and social services looking after his non-medical issues.

****** 70 ******

Why Wasn't It This Big When I Needed It?

An older man with excessive fluid retention was sitting in my office accompanied by his wife. His wife stated that the patient's private parts had grown, by quite a lot. After the initial interview regarding the patient's present and past medical history, it was determined that the patient was experiencing some kidney issues that resulted in this fluid retention and swelling. Upon examination of the patient, it became quite clear that both his penis and scrotum were drastically swollen. I ordered some medication and further tests, as well as an ultrasound of his kidneys; I told him to return in six weeks. Just before they left the office, the wife asked me, "Doctor, may I ask you a question?" I said sure. She said, "Why wasn't it this big when we were young? We could have used and enjoyed it more then than now, given we're old and less interested in sex?" I replied, "I don't have any answer," and they both laughed. I did mention to them that this was a disease-related enlargement and would have caused significant medical issues if it had occurred earlier in his life.

****** 71 ******

Which Finger Is Up?

A gentleman in his forties had been admitted to ICU where he had been intubated and was on mechanical ventilation. He was alert and awake and was approaching the time when his breathing tube could be removed. At this time, the telephone in the ICU rang and the patient's nurse picked it up and began talking to a person on the other end of the phone line, who was the patient's sister. Per HIPPA rules, the nurse asked the caller to identify herself and noted that this sister was *not* on the list of people who were eligible to be notified regarding the patient's condition. This list is usually provided by the patient upon admission. The nurse told the caller that although she believed that the caller was the patient's sister, she still could not release any information about the patient. The caller asked if the patient was awake and coherent. The nurse replied, "Yes he is, but he cannot talk to you." The caller asked the nurse to tell the patient that, "Your sister, Mary, is calling, and I love you and wish you a speedy recovery." The nurse relayed this message to the patient. In response, the patient raised his hand with the middle finger stretched upward. After seeing the patient's response, the nurse told his sister that she had given the massage to the patient and he showed a "thumb up." The sister asked that the nurse tell her the truth as they had not been on good terms. The nurse smiled and did not give a direct answer.

****** 72 ******

The Case of a Dark-Colored Worm

A colleague of mine showed me a picture of a dark brown worm that a woman had been passing in her stool for the past year or so and asked me if I could identify the worm. I looked at the picture and told her that I had never seen such a dark-colored worm in my life. He told me to ignore the color of the worm as the patient had been using coffee enemas, unsuccessfully he added, to kill the parasite. I jokingly asked my colleague if the patient had been using cream with her coffee as well or not? We both laughed.

****** 73 ******

Sudden Rise of Heart Rate on the ICU Monitor

A fifty-year-old man was admitted to ICU for a cardiac procedure. This patient had been placed on an order of nothing-by-mouth protocol for morning breakfast as he was scheduled to have the procedure. At seven am every day there's a change in shifts as the night staff clocks out and the day shift comes on. During this change over, the door for the patient's room was open but the curtain was pulled. His heart rate had been running around 75 all night and suddenly jumped up to 140, which caused the monitor alarm to go off. The nurses ran into the room and pulled back the curtain to catch him masturbating. I later told his cardiologist that since he didn't allow the patient to use his hands to eat, he had to use his hand for other purposes. The cardiologist replied that night shift had reported to him that this patient's heart rate had spiked last night as well. His wife, who was in the room with him at the time and behind the closed door, was using her mouth. But not for the purpose of eating.

****** 74 ******

Number 1.5

When I entered the room of my patient, an older Vietnamese woman, she was sitting on the commode trying to have bowel movement. She didn't speak English, but her daughter, who was in the room when I entered, was fluent in English. The daughter explained that the patient no longer had a problem with the passing number one (i.e., urine, which is what I was inquiring about given I am a nephrologist), but her mother was now experiencing a problem with going number two. I jokingly said, "Okay, ask her to have number one and half." The daughter started laughing loudly. The patient, who didn't understand what we were saying, thought that we were laughing at her. She was quite upset and angry, and began yelling at the daughter in their own language. The daughter translated my conversation with her to the mother, at which time the patient also started laughing.

****** 75 ******

Is It Raining Outside?

A mentally challenged young lady had been admitted to the hospital with an infection. Because the germ causing her infection was resistant to multiple antibiotics, the patient had been placed in isolation. Anyone entering her room had to wear a gown and gloves. When I arrived to see the patient, I was wearing the yellow gown and several of her family members were visiting her and were also wearing gowns. When I entered the room, she looked at me and after a while she asked if it was raining outside, assuming that we were wearing these gowns because of the rain. I had to explain to her the reason for the gowns.

****** 76 ******

Mental Tests for Awakening a Patient from a Recent Coma

A lady in her fifties and who had been in ICU and comatose for nearly ten days from an extensive infection finally opened her eyes. She was unable to follow simple commands and did not reply to any of my questions. When I called her name in a loud voice, she turned her head toward me. I said, "Do you have any pain?" She didn't respond. I said, "If you did not have any pain before, just looking at my ugly face should have caused you pain. Tell me, do you have any pain now?" She smiled, and I realized that she was still mentally intact. She recovered from her infection, returned to her baseline state, and was later discharged.

****** 77 ******

So Soft

One day I was wearing a suede jacket and holding my leather-covered folder. A nurse who was sitting at the nursing station next to me touched my folder cover, which was on the desk, and said, "Dr. Farb, this is so soft." I didn't reply. Then she touched my jacket and said, "This is also so soft." Again, I did not reply. Then she touched my hand saying, "Dr. Farb, even your hand is so soft." I had heard enough. I said, "Listen, when a man gets to my age, everything goes soft." She had a unique way of laughing. She sat on the floor holding her stomach, laughing continuously.

****** 78 ******

Dialysis Nurse Lecturing Two Older Gay Men

A male dialysis patient in his late sixties who had been admitted to the hospital with a blood infection was getting dialysis at the hospital. Another gentleman of similar age walked in to visit this patient. When the dialysis nurse asked the patient what kind of relationship the visiting gentleman had regarding this patient, he replied that this man was his husband. At that time, the dialysis nurse began preaching to them regarding Christianity. To make matters worse, it turns out that both men were Jewish, and the visitor was a lawyer. I had a hard time convincing them not to file a lawsuit.

****** 79 ******

A Lesson from My Dialysis Patient

I had an Armenian gentleman in his seventies as my patient who received dialysis three times a week. I used to visit him weekly at the dialysis center. He did not speak English, and I did not speak Armenian. We communicated in Turkish. One day after I finished visiting him and managing his medical issues, I was on my way out of the unit when he called me back. He said, "Doctor, I was reading a statement from a writer that there are only two things left behind of a person after he dies: his legacy and a piece of art or a book." Even though we did not have any related discussion that day to justify such a statement, I agreed with him. In fact, writing this book for me is in some way following his advice. After all, I can see the finish line on my marathon of life.

****** 80 ******

Various Issues with My Marathon Running Friend

I've had a few memorable issues related to my Marathon running friend who is now over 70 years old. He has worked very hard. As a result of his work and Marathon running, he has had a couple of interesting experiences.

We trained together when I was in Cleveland. He had a habit of coming to the hospital very early in the morning and not leaving until very late every day, sometimes on weekends as well. Once he completed his training, he started practicing at a prestigious place where he continued his old habit of going to work in dark and coming home late in the evening when it was dark. He continued with this pattern for several months, going between his house and the hospital when it was dark. One time when he was on vacation, he had to go to the hospital to get his paycheck. Even though he'd been going back and forth from his house to the hospital every day for seven months, this had always been in the dark. When he went to pick up his paycheck during the day, he got lost and was unable to find the hospital.

The second funny experience was after he'd become an established and very successful physician in California. One day, he was asked to give a lecture in Cleveland back at his old clinic. This was sometime in October. He called a friend in Cleveland, who also was a physician and was living in Cleveland, to ask if the weather were warm enough that he could continue with his marathon training while in Cleveland. The friend told him that the weather was relatively mild and insisted that when he came to Cleveland to stay at his house rather than go to a hotel.

The day after his arrival to Cleveland, he woke up very early in the morning and began his run. After he had run about three miles, he noticed that he didn't have much feeling between his legs. He took off his gloves to inspect his groin area; he had an extremely cold subject down there. Immediately after that, he began experiencing such severe pain that he was unable to run and, in fact, he hardly could walk. The pain was so severe that he had to crawl back to his friend's house. He was terrified that he might need to go to the emergency and that he'd make the local evening news. "Doctor from California Develops Frostbite on Certain Body Parts!" It took about two hours before he was able to get back to the house. When he finally made it back, his friend had already left for work. When he rang the doorbell, the friend's wife answered the door and demanded to know what was wrong. All he could say was to ask if she had a heating pad. Luckily, the frostbite was not severe, and he recovered without any permanent damage.

ADDITIONAL TALES

The followings are some of the stories that some of my colleagues experienced during their practice or studies.

****** 1 ******

Generosity of a Homeless Man

A nurse that I worked with at the hospital ran out of gas on her way home. It was a very wet day, and she did not have a raincoat or an umbrella. She got out of her car to walk to a nearby gas station was a homeless man sees her and assumed that she was homeless too as she is absolutely drenched. He runs over to her and covers her with his dirty jacket. She tells him that she is not homeless but was out walking in the rain to get gas for her car. She gave him some money to prove to him that she wasn't homeless and did have a job.

****** 2 ******

Prostate Check by Students in India

A colleague told me that when he was a medical student in India, a patient was admitted to the hospital with urine retention due to enlarged prostate. As soon as students found out about this patient, they all ran to his room to check his prostate by doing a rectal exam. The students were wearing the standard white coats. The following day in morning rounds, the attending staff was with the students, with all them wearing white coats when they entered the patient's room. The patient's son was with him as well. As soon as the patient saw the crowd, he started screaming and crying. His son said that he's afraid that all white coats wearing ones are going to do a rectal exam on him. The son asked the professor if that is the treatment that he should be having, then they can take him home and they can give him the same treatment at home by doing repeated rectal exams. Professor laughed and explained that he wouldn't have to undergo any more rectal exams by the students. They put a sign above the patient's bed which read, "No Rectal Exam."

****** 3 ******

Please Stand Up When You Ask Questions

In an amphitheater of a medical school, students were sitting in a circle of seats and their professor was lecturing from the bottom of the circle. When the professor finished with his lecture, he asked if there were any questions. A student said, "I have a question, sir." The professor said to the student, "Before you ask your question, let me remind you that it is more polite to stand up when you are addressing your teacher. Would you please stand up when you ask your questions?" The student replied, "But sir, I'm already standing." The professor, who was quite embarrassed laughed, and said, "You and I have the same problem as far as our height goes."

****** 4 ******

Dead Man Walking

In an Indian university hospital emergency room, a man walked in with a Foley catheter still in his bladder and yelled, "Take this damn thing out." He was asked who put the catheter in? He said, "You guys did." When they asked him his name and looked at the records, they couldn't find his name. They asked him if he had proof he had been treated at that hospital? He handed the ER doctor a piece of paper. The ER doctor realized that it was a death certificate of the very alive patient and had been signed by a physician who was the chief resident a few months ago but had finished his training and had left the hospital. They were able to locate his record and review it. Further questioning of the patient revealed that the patient had been admitted to this hospital a couple of months earlier with heart problems and had been in a coma. He had been on a ventilator and had had Foley catheter inserted to collect his urine as well as a nasogastric tube for feeding and medication use.

One night he began having recurrent episodes of cardiac arrhythmias due to ventricular tachycardia. He experienced repeated episodes of ventricular tachycardias and received numerous defibrillations to bring him back to life. Finally, close to midnight, the chief resident called the family and explained to them the situation and the high likelihood of death. The chief resident then told the supervisor on call that the patient's condition had been explained to the family, and that the family were removing him from the hospital so that he could die at home. The chief resident signed this man's death certificate and put next to the patient's bed. He then explained to the supervisor that when the family arrived, take out his breathing tube and let the family take him home. The family arrives and the supervisor does what was he told. They did not remove the feeding tube nor the catheter. They placed him on the back of a truck and took him home.

Although he was comatose, he could still breathe on his own. Over the next few days, he remained alive, and the family began feeding him milk through the feeding tube. Soon he regained consciousness. Eventually they removed the feeding tube and he continued to eat by mouth, but they were unable to remove the catheter. It was at this point that the patient had to eventually come to the emergency room to have the catheter removed. He had brought his death certificate to prove that he had been a patient there.

It became clear that an adverse reaction to medication had caused his irregular EKG and a prolongation of the QT interval, which made him to develop repeated episodes of ventricular tachycardia and cardiac arrest. This condition is called Torsades De Pointes and improves when the causative medications are discontinued, which is what happened on him when he was taken home to die. The Foley catheter has a balloon at the tip of it. After insertion, the balloon is inflated so it doesn't fall out. It cannot be removed until the balloon is deflated by a syringe or cutting the tail of the small, branched part of the catheter. The catheter was removed, and the patient discharged but not before they confiscated his death certificate and apologized for this mishap!!!

The End

CPSIA information can be obtained
at www.ICGtesting.com
Printed in the USA
BVHW040244021121
620535BV00013B/628